Investing Guide for Retirement

Build, Grow and Protect Your Financial Future

By Raymond M.F. Dominick

Library of Congress Control Number: 2015919122

ISBN – 13: 978-1519251084

ISBN – 10: 1519251084

Investment Solutions, LLC may be contacted at
PO Box 506, Bigfork, MT 59911 USA
investmentsolutionsmt@gmail.com

Table of Contents

INTRODUCTION: WHY YOU SHOULD BE MANAGING YOUR RETIREMENT *NOW*

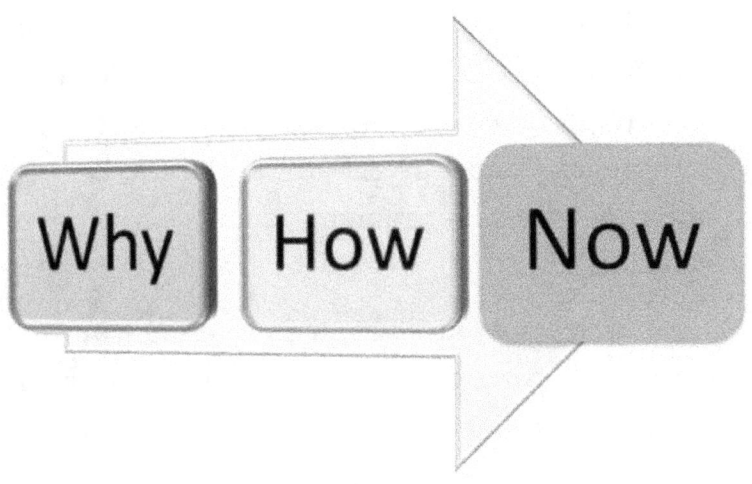

The day will come, if it hasn't already, when you will reach retirement age. When that day comes you will be faced with a new normal. For most of us, our survival will depend on being properly financially prepared. Most of us, me included, don't like to think about retirement from that perspective. When I was in my 40s retirement represented relaxing, traveling, and no more work stress. The importance of a retirement fund was not on my mental radar.

Since then I have learned there are many aspects to retirement: where to live, to own or rent, to work or not, securing enough medical coverage...but number one on the list is money, Money. Social Security benefits may help with the bills but is rarely enough to live on so a significant pension or large retirement account is a necessity to live comfortably and without worry. Yet the majority of Americans don't have ample retirement funds and many don't have any savings at all.

There are many aspects to retirement investing. As one friend noted, "The first thing that comes to mind is the importance of having that nest egg or those retirement funds in the first place...the importance of building that retirement fund while you are still working."

Failure to plan ahead is leaving your future up to chance. Waiting until retirement is looming will leave you with few options to build a retirement fund. More likely you will face your golden years in less than ideal circumstances:

- living on social security at or below the poverty level
- working until you can't—not very many businesses hire 70 or 80 year olds
- depending on your children to feed you

Here are two critical financial facts you will have to deal with before and during your retirement years: typically Social Security will account for 38 percent of your income when you retire and you will likely live at least 20 years after you retire; for many it will be 30-plus years.

Figuring out the size your retirement account needs to be to maintain your current standard of living is simple math:

.62 x (your current yearly income) x (the number of years you live after retirement) [this is a popular formula]

2

Plus, your retirement account must grow at a rate greater than inflation[1] just to stay even—that takes planning and strategy.

I am not an expert about where to live or how to evaluate retirement locations. And who am I to say whether or not you should work or play golf or join me on a hike in Glacier National Park. But I do know about investing as well as building and maintaining a retirement account. And I have experience on how to manage your retirement money so you can live without the stress of wondering how to pay this month's bills.

One of my passions is providing information, a blueprint if you will, about how retirement can be more than just survival. Retirement should be all about completing your life's dreams, sharing adventures, and living as you want. Establishing and managing a retirement account enables you to go from just surviving to enjoying life.

Getting started with a retirement account or managing your existing account involves knowing exactly what you have and what you need to do. Once you have a plan, it is critical to follow the best practices for safe investing. It doesn't do any good to create and grow a retirement account if you lose a chunk of it because the stock market hits one of its down cycles. You need to know how to protect yourself.

---

[1] The average historical rate is 3.22 percent.

Following the best practices means adopting proven investment strategies, not get rich quick schemes you see on late night infomercials or tips from your best friend. But don't be intimidated: it's actually pretty easy to diversify your money so it's not all in one vulnerable pot. You just have to be willing to spread your investing wings.

There are a zillion investing techniques and philosophies but most of us stick to what we've been doing rather than change or move forward. It seems every week a new book comes out touting another investing technique that people rush to buy but very few actually execute the new strategy. Use the cliché of your choice—we are creatures of habit, we prefer the devil we know, better safe than sorry—but trying something new can be scary. The desire to improve our return on investment is trumped by our fear of losing any of what we currently have.

But there is an even stronger impediment to realizing profitable investment results: fear of change. We get comfortable. Our life is good, or maybe even just okay. Sure, rent keeps climbing and the car insurance bill never goes down, but we make do by cutting back on something else to make ends meet—rather than change our investing approach.

I know there are people who make good money investing; you probably do to. But we assume it's because they have a lot of time to do it and that's not us. But becoming a part-time investor—even a very, very part-time investor—can cover the cost of rising gas prices or utility increases when you're retired and regular income disappears or declines. Most people believe keeping their body in shape is worth the several hours a week they invest in exercise. Investing in your financial future doesn't need to take much longer than a leisurely shower—and is much easier on your knees.

Chances are you're already an investor and don't really realize it. If you have an individual retirement account (IRA), a 401k plan at work, or a government retirement plan – a thrift savings plan (TSP), you are an investor. You do not need an MBA, or a college diploma, or a degree in mathematics to be a successful investor. You just need a bit of common sense, access to a computer, and a willingness to spend a couple hours a week—initially—to manage your own money.

If you have a retirement plan at work or an IRA that you established yourself, you can take control of your own destiny rather than letting some money manager who doesn't know you decide what's best for your financial future—and maybe lose chunks of your hard earned cash in the process.

In the pages ahead I want to give you a roadmap to your choices, the means to build your retirement account and keep it safe and growing so you will live a fulfilling retirement based on fulfillment, not a struggle for survival.

If you have not yet retired, this book will provide ideas on building a nest egg and investing safely so it doesn't disappear should the economy go sour. If you are already retired, this book covers 401ks, IRAs, Roth IRAs, and government thrift savings plans (TSP) so you can continue to grow your money with safe investment strategies that fit your personality.

The bottom line: you don't want your account to run dry while you're still breathing. And with our lifespans growing ever longer, long-term financial planning for retirement is more crucial than ever.

CHAPTER I: SAVING AND INVESTING FOR RETIREMENT

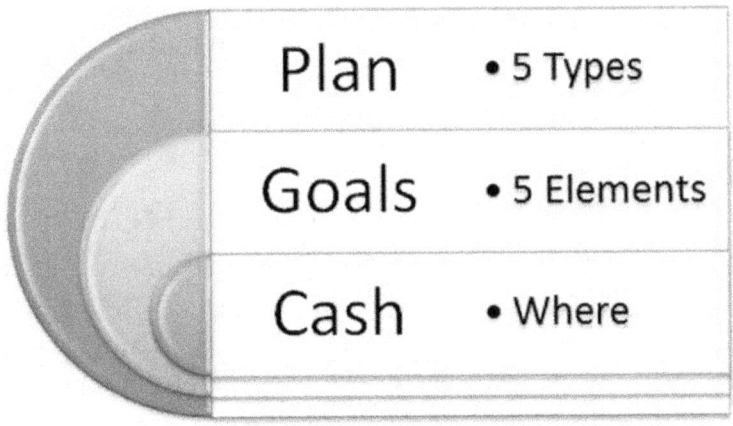

Investing and saving go hand-in-hand. For many people, their first investments are in safe options such as simple savings accounts. Getting into the habit of saving lays the foundation for later, more complex investments.

Too often young adults don't think to invest or build a retirement account. They wait until their late thirties or forties when they feel more established. The reality is young adults in their 20s have distinctive advantages to start saving and investing as soon as possible. If this is you consider:

- building a retirement account without panic
- taking advantage of time being on your side
- preparing to retire early

Take advantage of time being on your side. It is so much easier to put aside small amounts of money than having to dump hundreds upon hundreds out of every paycheck to bank enough for your later years.

Investing early gives you the wiggle room to make a few mistakes without it hurting your long term objectives and the time for a comfortable learning curve.

Your Key to Investing While Retired

There are certain principles, certain keys to investing if you are retired. Yes, there are many books on the subject and new magazine articles almost every month, but somehow they seem to either miss the key factors or their verbiage is so long the key points are glossed over.

It's kind of like when I go for a hike in Glacier National Park. What I want to know is:

What are the key characteristics of the trail?

What are the viewing highlights along the trail and at its destination?

What's the weather forecast?

What animals may I see?

Have there been bear sightings?

Because I'm not a scientist I don't want to know the geology every ten feet along the way, nor the name of every flower, and plant.

It's the same with managing your retirement funds. Concentrate on the key factors and then follow your trail map to success. As a retiree your keys to successful money management are:

- Am I interested in managing my investments myself or should I use a professional advisor/planner? This is a key to your trail. And do I have time – 20 minutes or more a week? If you are going to self-manage, what software program will you use?

- Do I prefer ETFs, or mutual funds or stocks? These are your viewing highlights and if you know how to classify or divide them into working groups, or have access to advice on this matter.

- Can you check your emotions at the door so you make unbiased decisions? Do market drops scare you like a lightning storm or can you shrug them off and keep on your trail because these are part of your ongoing weather forecast. Another aspect of your forecast is exactly that: what is your life expectancy? How long did your parents and grandparents enjoy life? Your investment diversification needs to be based on your life expectancy so you both earn and retain money for your trip down life's trail; being too conservative with a long life expectancy ahead could result in a money shortage down the road while being too aggressive may risk your core too much.

- Are you easily distracted by news, comments or suggestions from friends that may sway you to buy or sell? These are the animal sightings that can distract you along the way, even as they are captivating at the same time.

- Do your strategies encompass signals for when to take safe cover, such as when there is a major market drop? Seeing grizzly bears in the wild is awesome, but preferably from a distance and if up close with bear spray in hand and knowledge of how to react to a bluffing or charging bear. You need the same safety plans when investing.

Investing in retirement can be daunting and even scary, but following certain principles will allow you to manage your retirement account profitably. From online brokers to magazines and a multitude of websites there are both plenty of resources and challenges.

Successful investing for retirement involves (1) diversification; (2) getting recommendations on when to buy and sell based on comparisons with the overall market, other stocks, or mutual funds; and (3) learning market exit signals.

Cooking Up a Fantastic Retirement

Here's another way to look at your retirement:

Are you a chef? Or perhaps a baker or maybe you like to tinker in a shop. Maybe you're a photographer and you enjoy editing and enhancing your photographs.

If you are also an investor or just want to manage your retirement account you have a lot in common with chefs, bakers, photographers and anyone working on a project.

The common factor is The Recipe.

10

Cakes, fudge, peanut butter cookies, encrusted chicken breasts; none of these turn out very well if you don't follow the recipe. And it can be extremely difficult to build a bookcase or edit a photo if you skip step two in the rush to get finished – at least if you want a quality result.

Investing is exactly the same. Success comes from following a recipe. You can't meet your retirement goals if your skip parts of your investing recipe.

Just like baking or building a bookcase you need ingredients and a plan or sequence of action.

Elements of an Investing Recipe

Building and maintaining a successful retirement account requires a few key ingredients and a plan on how to use these ingredients:

- What – are you going to invest in stocks, ETFs or mutual funds; or maybe some of each
- How – how are you going to make your buy – sell decisions; investment software, newsletters or use an investment advisor.
- When – will you make decisions daily, weekly or perhaps monthly?

The challenging part is to follow your recipe. This sounds easy, but this is where most folks get tripped up.

If you decide to work with an investment advisor, once you have agreed upon how you want your portfolio handled you have to let him do it. Calling him every day or even every week to ask 'why" he bought or didn't buy or sell something isn't letting the advisor do his job – you are not following the recipe.

The same thing applies to using investing software. You may develop strategies by back-testing or optimizing buy-sell rules to meet your particular goals. Once you have strategies that you like – good results, acceptable losses, then it is time to follow the recommendations.

If you tinker with your investment software recommendations then you are not following the recipe. You will not succeed. This is especially true if you look at a strong recommendation and then look to find fault with it. In effect you are not just ignoring your recipe but discarding the back-testing that led to your proven investment strategy.

So yes, investing and taking care of your retirement account is just like making peanut butter cookies. If you leave out half the peanut butter the recipe is just not going to work.

Choosing a Retirement Plan

As I said, your investment diversification needs to be based on your life expectancy so you both earn and retain money for your trip down life's trail; being too conservative with a long life expectancy ahead could result in a money shortage down the road while being too aggressive may risk your core too much.

There are five basic types of investment retirement accounts which I will discuss in detail in Chapter 4, but here are the five basic types:

- *A regular stock/fund investment trading account*
- *A 401(k)* or similar employer offered retirement account
- *Traditional IRA.*
- *Roth IRA.*
- *Annuity.*

If you have a 401(k) account at work, you should still consider opening a Roth IRA to bolster your financial future. Regardless of what type of account you have, if you are willing to spend at least a few hours once a month or better yet 20 minutes a week to oversee your investments, they will be more secure and grow substantially larger.

Money Management

As a retiree there are several keys to successful money management. The first is deciding if you are going to manage your investments or use a professional advisor. If you are going to self-manage, do you have 20 minutes or more a week to devote to it? Can you check your emotions at the door so you make unbiased decisions? Again, do market drops scare you like a lightning storm or can you shrug them off and keep on with life because these are part of your ongoing weather forecast.

Taking control of your financial future is no different than handling your everyday finances. Most of us pay our bills once a week, or twice a month, maybe just monthly, but we pay them on a regular schedule that fits our lifestyle and personal time constraints. *Managing your retirement* is just the same.

You can actually simplify the management of your retirement without giving up control if you follow certain key principles:

- recognize your retirement future
- define how to manage your retirement
- confirm your time
- establish a method
- keep your focus
- recognize your retirement future

Recognizing means taking stock of what you have and writing down where you want your retirement account to be. Sure, you may have a 401k or an IRA but that doesn't mean you really, truly have recognized its importance to your future. The fact that a retirement account exists is only part of the recognition. The other part is knowing or planning what you want from your account. This means thinking about how much money you will need in the future because even with Social Security you will need a lot more money to live the way you do now, and even more than that to travel or enjoy other luxuries.

Once you are on your path to taking control of your retirement future it is essential to keep your focus and develop a habit of checking your portfolio. This doesn't mean you have to look at every day or become obsessed with it. All you need, with the right investment software, is 20 minutes a week or even every month. The key is to establish a habit.

Setting Your Investment Goals

Defining your investment goals requires more than just saying: *I want to make money.* It requires an honest assessment of:

Your personality. Are you a risk taker? Are you willing to lose money in order to make money? In other words, if you were managing a baseball team how likely would it be for you to call for a squeeze bunt play? Or would you go with a friend for an all day hike in the back country of Glacier National Park, famous for its stunning mountain vistas—and grizzly bears? In other words, determine whether you are more likely to be a conservative or an aggressive investor, or whether your personality falls somewhere in between.

Time. Be honest about how much time you can—or will-devote to your investments. If work, family, and pastimes chew up most of your time you may only have a half hour a week. If there are not many demands on your time you may have 20 minutes every day.

An aggressive investor will make time almost every day to make investment decisions while a conservative investor may be comfortable spending just a half hour a week or maybe even just every other week reviewing their portfolio. Moderate investors, like myself, typically only need 20 minutes a week.

Current resources. If you have minimal resources, aggressive goals may need to be handled carefully so as not to endanger your cash and future growth. This doesn't mean you have to take a totally conservative investment

15

stance, just that you may need to balance or have multiple goals.

Future resources. Building your retirement portfolio with additional cash each week or month can allow you to pursue more moderate or aggressive goals because your investment base is growing.

Profit uses. How you plan on using your investment profits is an important consideration. How soon you want to reach a certain cash level can push you towards either a conservative, aggressive, or middle of the road approach in making your decisions.

Combining your honest answers to these five aspects of developing your retirement and goals should help you focus on the investment method that works best for you. You should write down the answers so that you keep your focus and don't allow one-time events or conversations sway you off track.

Failure to define your goals will result in not achieving the retirement lifestyle you deserve and need.

How You Can Find Cash to Invest

Finding cash to invest is a challenge for many people but they are strategies that can help. Many pundits say you just need to give up "small" things every day or week and that will give you more cash. But my experience is that those who drink that cup of latte every morning on the way to work depend on that drink to get them going, so while eliminating the latte may put a few bucks in the wallet, it may also affect your daily performance in the wrong way.

Many years ago I heard the phrase *pay yourself first* and it has been repeated in articles on a consistent basis. *Easier said than done*, I told myself every time I heard it. But then one day, the vice president of a major company told me how to pay myself first in a way that made it easy on my wallet. Here are my suggestions:

• Use an online, internet based savings account.
• Take advantage of an employer based retirement account.
• Open a regular savings account at a nearby credit union or bank.

Don't throw your arms up in exasperation because you've heard this before and it never worked. The following method does.

The critical aspect of gathering cash for investment is it has to be specifically aimed at putting together money for investing then ultimately your cash will grow significantly when it is invested in stocks, ETFs, or mutual funds. The savings account is a temporary parking place for your money because while it may grow in value, the interest earnings are very minor.

Generally speaking, an online savings account will earn substantially more money than at a bank and even more than at most credit unions. Today one of my online savings accounts is paying 1.2 percent while my friend's credit union account is only paying 0.02 percent.

Depending upon whether you want to invest in stocks, ETFS, or mutual funds you need $100 to $2,500 to get going, depending on the brokerage you choose and the type of investment. Additional investments, once you have an account open, are best made in increments of no less than $500.

For this reason the savings account should be dedicated to accumulating dollars for your retirement years. In other words, it is a separate savings account from any other account you may have. You can do this by starting out very slowly and building. The key is to set the investment retirement account up for automatic deduction from your checking account into a high interest paying savings account. Let's say you make $30,000 a year and your net take home pay is $850 every two weeks or about $1,700 a month. Start with an automatic deduction that is equal to 1 percent of your take home pay; in this case $17. You won't even notice it.

After two or three months change your automatic deduction to 2 percent; in this case $34 and again, because you will only be taking out another $17 from your checking account every month than what you're used to, you won't miss it. If you get paid every two weeks you could set up the deduction for twice a month, in this case just $8.50 to start. Every three months increase your automatic deduction. Try to get it up to 10 percent or even better 15 percent.

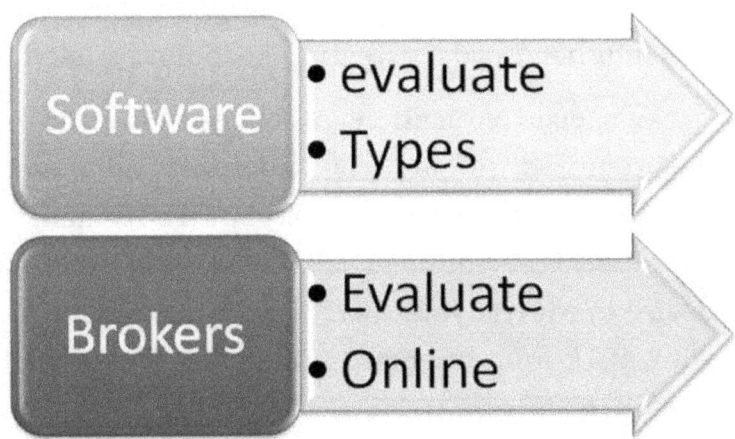

Success in investing requires both persistence and trust. All investing is a bet on the future. The difference is how you arrive at your bet.

Hunches. A hunch is based on what we think we know and not on research or analysis. I don't recommend this method.

Tips. A suggestion from a friend, co-worker, investment expert, or the Internet. Very Questionable.

Media. Business TV shows, Internet articles and forums, magazines and newspapers. Without knowing their batting average, these recommendations may not have any more value than an ordinary tip.

Fundamental Research and Analysis. You can do it yourself or read someone else's reports about the management of a stock or fund, the industry, and product trends and viability along with their financial status. Decision making based on fundamentals is primarily for long-term investing because a thorough analysis can take days, weeks, and even months.

In other words, investing need not be a bet.

A special education, a college degree in business, is not required to pay your monthly bills, nor are they required to take control of your retirement account or your ability to build wealth. All that is required is the desire to control your own destiny and finances. Managing your 401k and other investments are easy with the right tools.

It's natural to be afraid of risking your money. No one wants to lose anything, much less money and especially a life's savings. But money under the mattress will only be worth half of its current value after 20 or 40 years. The only way to have the money you need for retirement is to invest safely and profitably. And as with most things, there are tools available that can help your efforts.

Just as remodeling a home requires materials, know-how, and the right tools, the same is required for building a successful retirement portfolio.

Hardware

A computer or tablet with Internet connectivity will enable you to manage your investments. There are also smart phone apps you can use.

Online Broker Accounts

There are many user friendly online brokers like Fidelity, Schwab, and TD Ameritrade that let you open an account with almost any amount of money. And you can easily move accounts from one broker to another.

Investment Software

Most investment software programs are entirely chart based—which can involve a long learning curve—but some are based on technical analysis while a few combine both analysis and charts.

Chart analysis. Reading charts can provide you with indications or indicators of future performance based on past performance of a ticker symbol. There are free Internet chart services as well as pay services. It can be challenging learning a chart program. However, even with very user-friendly software you may still have questions. So it is important to have access to real-time support.

Technical analysis. Evaluating the data of a particular ticker symbol or group of symbols can produce charts, spreadsheet results, or reports based on the analysis. Chart analysis is a type of technical analysis but a true technical analysis program goes further by allowing you to evaluate the symbol or group data in additional ways and provide clearly prepared reports that make decision making easier. Depending upon your objectives and time frame these software programs can involve as little as 20 minutes a week and provide reliable investing recommendations.

Personally I like to use technical analysis that gives me an easy to read report coupled with key charts that can confirm recommendations. Key charts like moving average and full stochastic[2] can be especially helpful when the markets are volatile and jumping up and down from day to day or week to week. Investment software that lets you analyze based on different types of relative strength investing is critical.

How to Evaluate Investment Software

A number of key factors should be considered when evaluating investment analysis software. These include price, but price is not necessarily a good determining factor. Important factors in choosing an investment program include:

- deciding what type works best for you;
- any money-back guarantees;
- what kind of training is available;
- what kind of personal support is available;
- cost.

I recommend software that is comprehensive yet easy to learn and doesn't require hours of time. Comprehensive investment software lets you pick a method of analysis and then gives both recommendations and charts for what to buy from a group or universe of funds, ETFs, or stocks, *plus* when to sell based upon different criteria. This type software usually has an optimization or back test feature to find the best buy/sell rules that meet your goals and desires.

---

[2] Randomly determined; having a random probability distribution or pattern that may be analyzed statistically but may not be predicted precisely.

Comprehensive software often also:

    • provides a signal that says now is the time to exit or enter the markets

    • gives the option of examining individual ticker symbol data and comparing the data   with other tickers.

    • gives you an easy to read screen or report of all your investment positions

    • provides the opportunity to back-test different investment models or strategies to find what works best for the ticker symbols available in your retirement account

There are a few magazines that cover investing, over a thousand books with all kinds of advice, and many blogs. These can be more confusing than anything, but it's important to see if the investment program you choose also posts a blog with tips about their software so you get the most out of the program.

Selecting an Online Broker

All online brokers want your money, but it's important to choose one that you feel comfortable with. Every year magazines like *Kiplinger's* and *Money* rate the various online brokers for ease of use, cost, and other criteria. But just because someone else says this is the way to go doesn't mean that broker will work for you. I suggest you do a little homework.

There are many online brokers to choose from but I suggest you start with these:

Fidelity Investments, http://personal.fidelity.com

eTrade, https://us.etrade.com

TD Ameritrade, www.tdameritrade.com

CharlesSchwab, www.schwab.com

Scottrade, www.scottrade.com

Remember that you are buying their services. *They* will be working for *you*, not the other way around. So you want their site to be easy and do the things you want to do. Also, depending upon how much money you have to invest and how frequently you trade, they may have an advance trading site that is even more comprehensive or easier to use; Fidelity calls theirs, *Fidelity Active Trade Pro*."

When comparing brokers, here are some factors to consider:

Initial fee to open an account. This amount is usually different for a regular account versus a retirement account. For example, Fidelity wants $2,500 for all accounts but they will waive the minimum for a retirement account with regular automatic contributions. Scottrade only requires $500 to open an account.

Trading fees. This can be different depending upon whether you are investing in stocks, ETFS, and mutual funds. Fees are only one aspect in choosing a broker so don't make this the deciding factor.

Screens and reports. How user-friendly is the website and what kinds of reports will you get? Plus, can you easily find the reports and anything else you look for?

Availability. Not all ETFs, mutual funds, or stocks that may interest you are always available. Also, some sites may charge more than others for certain funds or ETFs.

Customer service. Email the same question to all the brokerages you are considering and see what kind of response you get:

Interface. Can you manage more than one account on just one screen? Just as you should have multiple savings accounts, you should also have multiple investment accounts. You should have a retirement account, a wealth building account, and perhaps a vacation account. Plus, if you are married, see if you can manage your spouse's account from your screen without having to log off and then login to their account. This could be your question to email.

Record keeping. Do they keep records for tax purposes or do you need to keep and track everything?

Mutual funds. If you plan on investing in funds, find out their rules on round-trips and short-term trading fees. (I discuss these in another chapter.)

Remember, the brokers want your business. But also remember that it is your money and you want them to work your way.

Rise above the Crowd with Profitable Investing

The Pareto principle, popularly known as the 80/20 rule, states that for many events roughly 80 percent of the effects come from 20 percent of the causes. For example,

20 percent of your work consumes 80 percent of your time and resources. Twenty percent of customers account for 80 percent of sales. And 80 percent of a company's inventory comes from 20 percent of its suppliers.

Pareto's principle can also be applied to investing. Eighty percent of investment earnings will be accrued by 20 percent of investors. You can be in that top 20 percent of all investors—probably in the top 5 percent of people—and you can do it with safe investing methods in less than 20 minutes a week.

The primary difference between those that rise above the crowd and record fantastic gains is exactly because they don't follow the crowd—and neither should you. Crowd followers with retirement accounts lost their shirt when our Great Recession hit back in 2008.

Non-investors—people who don't even invest in stocks, ETFs, or mutual funds—form the biggest crowd yet. Hopefully you're not one of them, and when the market soared in 2009-2010 their bank accounts were just as empty as ever.

An investment program with the best investment tools can help you be a winner and not just a follower. But the biggest and most important reason that these tools allow you to rise above the crowd is simply your decision to do so. There is no secret trick, no secret path, no special requirement—*just the decision to invest safely and profitably.*

If our recent recession proved anything, it's that all the advocates of patterned investing were wrong. Investing based strictly on buy and hold forever rarely produces strong gains and only exposes you to major losses. Investing based on allocation of your money simply according to your age exposes you to major losses when you are young and denies you the opportunity to score profits when you are older. A lose-lose concept.

If you are determined to rise above the crowd and be one of the 20 percent, not a crowd follower, find an investing tool and maximize its capabilities. You will not only succeed but far surpass those who simply follow. Yes, you will have to be actively involved in your future, in handling your money, but why not reach your goals and leave the crowd behind? It's like finishing a marathon at the front versus somewhere buried in the middle.

CHAPTER 3: KEY PRINCIPLES OF SAFE INVESTING

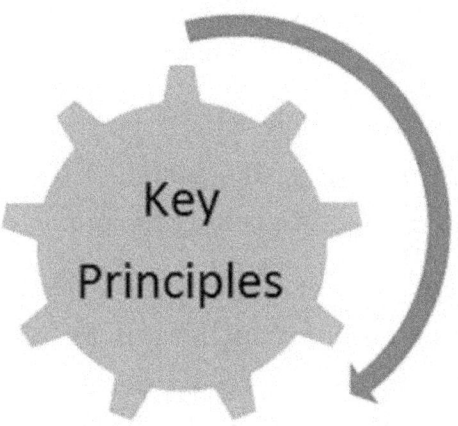

Building your retirement account safely doesn't mean you have to be a conservative investor, although you may still want to designate a portion of your portfolio for conservative investing, which may not make you super rich overnight but will preserve your cash. I don't know about you, but I don't want investing to be a gamble; especially for my retirement. I want to know where my money is going and how it may grow, even if just a little. I suspect you are with me on this.

Safe investing may sound like an oxymoron to many, but investing need not be a crap shoot if certain simple, common sense principles are followed. However, even safe investing is not risk-free and there may be losses along the road to increased wealth and a secure retirement.

It's like driving: Some roads have just been built or resurfaced and are totally smooth, easy to drive, just like there are new stocks, ETFs or funds. Then there are roads that are bumpy, cracked, and filled with potholes that can bust a tire, break an axel, or tear off an oil pan.

Investing can be just as risky—or safe—as driving.

Here are a few key principles to keep your retirement account safe:

- Determine how much you are willing to risk your money. It's just like deciding what roads you would prefer to avoid.

- Identify the types of investments you consider safe for either all or part of your money. This could be dividend-paying stocks, funds, ETFs, and bonds, or funds and ETFs that are indexed or follow certain industries or economic sectors.

- Be realistic about how much time you are willing or able to put into managing your money for its future growth. If you are can spend 30–60 minutes every day, you can become a best performer almost instantly. If your obligations only allow you about 20 minutes once a week, then your investment process should be based on technical analyses that gives weekly buy-and-sell signals that meet your *willingness of risk*. If your time is very limited and you only want to spend an hour every month or two, then you can still do so.

- Just as detours and road closures can change the route we take to a store, be prepared to change course with your investments. Perhaps today you only want to spend an hour every few months managing your portfolio, but in the future you may switch to weekly management. If you are going to use a software program to help manage or make investment decisions, be sure the program is flexible enough to allow you to switch course when you want.

• Develop an exit strategy, a signal that tells you when to cash out to preserve your money against market crashes or bounces. It's just like knowing what freeway exit to use when you see that sign saying *Construction Ahead.*

Safe, conservative investment requires a bit of discipline. You have to remember that you are investing for the long term, for your retirement years, and a one-day drop in the markets is no reason to panic and sell. In contrast, a sustaining market decline could be reason to re-examine your positions. But if your positions are all producing strong income and are the type to come back after a decline, then decide carefully whether or not to sell. When you do sell in a market downturn, a conservative attitude would be to move either to cash or into more bond positions.

Do not allow yourself to be swayed into risky or aggressive investments. This may seem logical, but we humans are emotional beings and susceptible to rash decisions. Remember: a safe, conservative portfolio or subportfolio of all your investments is an important strategy for securing your money for the future.

Three-Step Plan for Safe Investing

Verifying that what you are about to buy for an investment actually has a great probability of going up and making you money is an important element of stock investing. If you are concerned about managing risk, about safe investing and maintaining your cash base through market ups and downs this three-step plan will help you achieve your retirement goals.

Of course, the same holds true for buying ETFs or mutual funds. The greater your confidence in your investment selection the more likely it is to be a winner.

Analyzing is the process of evaluating my groups according to a specific means of technical analysis. I normally use alpha or relative strength momentum, but you can use any type of analysis including:

 • Alpha is a measure of the so-called active return on an investment, the performance of that investment compared to a suitable market index.

 • The relative strength index (RSI) is a technical indicator used in the analysis of financial markets. It is intended to chart the current and historical strength or weakness of a stock or market based on the closing prices of a recent trading period.

 • Return on investment (ROI) is the benefit to the investor resulting from an investment

of some resource. A high ROI means the
investment gains compare favorably to
investment cost

You can also add standard deviation—a measure of the
investment's volatility—to whatever method you use.

Once your computer has found the best ticker symbol
to buy based on analysis verify that the symbol chosen is
in fact ranked better than the index or benchmark you are
using for comparison purposes. If the symbol is not
performing better than the benchmark then it is likely
going down and you would lose money. So don't buy it. I
also like to see that the particular symbol is ranked near
or at the top of the list of all my symbols in the particular
group.

Verifying the strategy is making sure that the
overall strategy—with its buy analysis and rules for
selling—are profitable. Trading strategies can be
profitable some of the time while not productive at other
times; this is normal.

I use two charts in particular to verify the
effectiveness of my trading strategies. You can make your
own choices, but mine are moving average and full
stochastic.

In the moving average chart, I want to see that the
price line for the recommended symbol is above both the
slow and the fast moving averages. This would be a *buy* or
hold signal. In between the lines is a *maybe* or *watch me*

signal. If the price line is below both moving average lines, then that is a *don't buy* or *sell* signal.

Reading the full stochastic chart is a bit trickier. Here I look to see if the stochastic line is above the trigger line. When this occurs in the lower fifth of the chart it is a *buy* signal; when above the upper fifth, it is a *hold* and possible *buy* signal. When the stochastic line cuts down thru the trigger line in the upper fifth of the chart it is a *sell* or *don't buy* signal.

The best *buy* signal is when both charts are signaling *buy*, but occasionally one chart will say *buy* while the other is neutral or *maybe*. I may buy in this situation depending upon step three.

Verifying the ticker is critical to be sure its movement is positive. I look at the same chart types for the particular selected tickers as I did for the strategy: moving average and full stochastic.

With the ticker, I want to see a *buy* signal in the charts. Sometimes between the four charts I may have just two or three *buy* signals. Four is obviously best but with three and with the fourth chart heading towards a *buy* signal it is usually safe to go with that selection.

Implementing this three-step plan sounds more complicated than it is. I can go through the entire process for a dozen strategies in 15 minutes or less. And actually, there is software that now automates this process and shows you the results in just a few moments.

The Key Principles of Safe Investing

There are books galore on safe investing for retirement but it revolves around three key principles, that if followed will help your long-term investment become quite profitable and help give you a nice, comfortable retirement.

Consistency. Successful investing requires consistency. Just like good dental practice means brushing your teeth every day, profitable investing requires a consistent method, a stick-to-itiveness that doesn't change with the blowing of the wind or even a sudden storm.

Consistency goes hand in hand with routine. Whether you work on managing your retirement portfolio once a week or daily or even once a month it should be done about the same time day after day or week after week. Similarly, safe investing decisions require using the same method each time you sit down to evaluate your portfolio and decide where to place your money. This means sticking with one investment software program, for example, and not jumping from your program to taking advice from a magazine columnist, newsletter, or TV commentator. It's one or the other, all the time.

Proven analysis. There are many ways to analyze the markets or groups of stocks, ETFs or mutual funds. The key here is to use the same types of analysis proven to work with the types of investments you want and for the goals you seek. Again, such analysis may include:

• relative strength momentum

- alpha analysis
- return analysis
- specific charts
- buy/sell rules

Some of these may work best for stocks, others for mutual funds or ETFs. Be that as it may, stick with the one or two that work best for the type of investment you are considering. If for example your retirement account is all mutual funds, then stick with alpha or relative strength momentum analysis.

Simplicity. Picking what stocks or funds in which to place your money doesn't have to be complicated.

Choices can be made from groups of funds, ETFs, or stocks that already exist. It isn't necessary to reinvent the wheel or try to figure out which stock from amongst the thousands on the markets is best today. There are dozens of such pre-existing groups including:

- select funds, like Fidelity Selects
- sector ETFS or funds
- asset funds or ETFS
- large cap (big companies) stocks
- dividend paying stocks

If you narrow your search for the best place to put your money to pre-existing groups and use a proven means of analysis coupled with tested buy/sell rules, your chances of strong profits with minimal losses will become immense. Use these principles with consistency and your will have a growing retirement nest egg.

Safe Investing with Stops

Protecting your investment money can be a challenge. There are strategies you can use to follow a path of safe investing. The most common is to set *stops* that trigger an automatic sell of your holdings whenever the particular stock, fund, or ETF drops a pre-specified amount.

Almost everyone has heard of, or uses trading stops to prevent investment losses. But have you considered the key ramifications of how you use stops?

Traders know they can put a "trailing (or high) stop" on a position with either a set dollar figure or a percentage. So the questions start with how do *you* decide what amount or percentage. But this is just the starting question because there are more; in fact here are the questions to consider in using stops:

- Why use stops
- What type stops
- Are all stops equal

Why use stops – the common answer is to protect yourself from losses. But there are more reasons. I like to think of stops as having three functions:

- Stops lock in my profits so that when an ETF starts to drop from its high point I still make money. This way if the ETF is climbing and then starts to drop I know I am still going to make a profit because I'll get a sell signal or automatic trade based on the percentage drop from the greatest high the ETF reached since I purchased it.

- Stops prevent me from losing too much money when I set a stop below my purchase price. I may want a 3% or 5% stop below what I paid for the stock so if it tumbles my risk is limited to just that amount.
- Stops help control my trading frequency if I set them based on the type of ticker symbol, the type of group the position comes from, and how often I prefer to trade. In other words a tight stop of just a few percentage points is going to result in more frequent trading while a higher number, say 7% or 9% will result in fewer trades and perhaps less volatility in my portfolio.

What type stops – you have a choice between using a set dollar figure or a sliding figure based on percentage. The set figure works great or just as well for a stop based on the purchase price to minimize your risk of losing money. But unless you want to be constantly updating your stop a set figure doesn't work very well for a trailing or high stop; in this case a percentage based stop is the best way to go.

Are all stops equal – stops have multiple influences besides just being a point at which you may sell a position.

The personality of your strategy or group, the characteristics of the individual ticker symbol can all have an influence on what setting can or should be used. An ETF that bounces around a lot, but within a tight range would lead you to frequent and possibly unnecessary trading if you had tight stops like 2, 3 or even 4% whereas stops of 6% to 9% will still allow you to lock in profits but avoid the frequent trades.

If however, you want to trade frequently, minimize risk and make money on small profits then tight stops make absolute sense.

There is a pitfall to using automatic stops that kick in with your broker. There is no guarantee your position will actually sell at your stop price because if the markets are extremely volatile or there is a shortage of buyers you could find yourself selling for a substantially lower amount. This is why some investors simply have their investment program give them sell signals which can be based partially on stops so they can pick the time to sell.

In any event, to totally ignore stops would be dangerous because you are putting your retirement monies at risk without any warning device to help you preserve your original money or your profits.

So how you setup stops and how or when you implement them is a matter of personal outlook and philosophy. The choices include:

- *Percent or actual basis*. A *percentage stop* means that if the price of the investment drops X percent a sell signal is generated; whereas an *actual stop* generates a sell signal when the price drops a specific amount (i.e. 50 cents).

- *Broker activated*. Stops set with your online broker or representative will kick-in automatically. Understand, however, that doesn't mean a sale will occur exactly when your stop is triggered because prices can change fast or the brokerage can be swamped with sell orders that can easily result in a different sell price when the order is actually executed.

• *Strategy activated*. This is a signal generated by an investment program trading strategy that then recommends selling and possibly purchasing a different position. Depending upon the strategy this can occur daily, weekly, or just monthly.

Various questions arise about how to actually implement stops and if one technique is better than others. In most situations many investors will simply execute or have their broker automatically execute the stops. But if the downturn was a one-day or short-lived price drop the stock may rebound above the stop so if the stop was executed it unnecessarily removed you from holding that position.

If a weekly strategy is followed, a price drop mid-week may end up being ignored by the stop signal because the stock rebounded before the close of the week. If an automatic stop-trade was executed then you either have to buy the position back—which may not be possible in the case of most mutual funds—or wait until a new sell-buy signal is generated in the future.

On the other hand, if the ticker is dropping daily and the stop signal is ignored until the end of the week for a weekly strategy, the drop could be more than the actual stop. Even so, weekly trading strategies have proven to be highly successful. Surveys indicate that weekly traders are just as likely to have the same results as the vast majority of end-of-day traders. Only a very small minority of end-of-day trading strategies have greater returns than weekly or even occasional trading strategies.

Using Charts for Safe Profitable Investing

Charts are a popular way to make stock trading decisions, but which ones you use and how you configure them is critical to matching your goals and objectives. The danger in using charts is that you can become overwhelmed. The challenge with charts is the individual chart settings. Most online sources, even brokerages, have default settings. But who benefits with these default settings?

The real objective in using charts is to tell you when to sell, hold a position, or buy a new stock or fund. Sounds simple enough, but do these signals meet with your objectives for growth, the frequency you are willing to trade, or look at your portfolio or level of risk tolerance?

I discussed this a bit as part of my three-step plan, but let me review this once more. For example, let's look at a moving average chart, which typically shows a fast (F) average (the average price calculated over a short time period), and a slow (S) average (the average price calculated over a longer time). In addition, there is also the actual total return price line of the particular stock or fund.

Conventional evaluation of a moving average chart is that if the price line cuts down through both the fast and slow lines that is a *sell* signal. Conversely, when it cuts up through both lines it is a buy signal and when it is in the middle it is either a *watch* signal if you are considering buying this or a *hold* signal if you already own the stock.

In another example, the full stochastic chart can also be used to give buy-hold-sell signals. This chart typically shows an average price line calculated from two types of moving averages (K + D) and a trigger line (T). When the average price line crosses the trigger signals are generated.

In general with a full stochastic chart, when the price line cuts **up** through the trigger line and is in the **bottom** 20 percent area of the chart, it is a *buy* signal; when the price line cuts **down** through the trigger line and is in the **top** 20 percent area of the chart, it is a *sell* signal. When the price line is between the bottom 20 percent and the top 20 percent it is in *watch* territory. Monitor it for a few days before taking any action, if at all.

These charts do not always agree with each other, which is great because it makes me look hard rather than just glance, and I can still make a decision in less than 30 seconds. Remember, I just use the charts to confirm or rule out the results of the technical analysis provided by my investment program.

Again, the key to using charts is to set them up to meet your personal objectives and to use only those charts that you feel comfortable using.

Creating a retirement account can be daunting. So let's discuss this further.

A plethora of articles, books, and websites are all jostling to advise you which way to turn and what is best for you, as long as you're willing to wade through hundreds of pages or hours of videos. I am going to keep this discussion simple yet comprehensive enough so that you can make a sound decision on developing your retirement account for investing in your future.

Remember, I said your investment diversification needs to be based on your life expectancy, so you both earn and retain money for your trip down life's trail; being too conservative with a long life expectancy ahead could result in a money shortage down the road while being too aggressive may risk your core too much.

The Five Basic Types of Investment Retirement Accounts

A regular stock/fund investment trading account. This account can provide cash for both your future retirement years and current times. The downfall: there are no tax advantages whatsoever.

401(k) or similar employer offered retirement account. These accounts have a few advantages:

- Your employer may provide matching or partially matching money for every dollar you put in for your retirement, so not taking advantage of this is like turning down a pay raise.

- The money you put in is not taxable when you put it in.

- In a pinch you may be able to borrow some of this money (and immediately start making payments).

The disadvantages include:

- You may get taxed on what you put in and however much additional money has accrued when you withdraw during retirement.

- Early withdrawal triggers penalties plus taxes.

- Switching jobs while you have a loan against your 401k can trigger either full loan repayment or massive taxes and penalties.

Traditional IRA. This account is similar to a 401(k) except it is entirely self-funded and you set it up yourself with the broker of your choice. Also, the annual limit to how much you can put into your IRA is more limited than with a 401(k). The downsides are similar to a 401(k). But while you cannot technically borrow against the account, there is a way to make a series of early withdrawals without penalty. With this type account you are required to make withdrawals at age 70, no matter what. If you really want to lower your present tax bill and are going to put in hundreds of dollars each month then a traditional IRA may be best for you. You will still pay the tax man when you take out your money along with its earnings.

Roth IRA. This type of retirement account has many differences from the traditional IRA. While it is also self-created with the same contribution limit of a traditional IRA, a Roth IRA does not provide an immediate tax deduction on your contribution; you pay taxes on that money just like normal. But when you go to withdraw your money there are no taxes on your original investment or its earnings and growth, which should be substantial.

There are provision in the Roth IRA rules that allow you to make early withdraws of the money you put in without penalties; but if you take out earnings then you get hit with taxes and penalties. So, if you don't mind paying your income taxes upfront (like you already are) then the rewards from a Roth IRA will be awesome because all the earnings/growth are tax free once you hit retirement age and decide to make withdrawals. So even if you have a 401(k) account at work, you should still consider opening a Roth IRA to bolster your financial future.

Annuity. An annuity is a life insurance type of account that can provide a set payout amount or set earnings until payout. Contributions are usually taxable but the income is usually tax free. There are many varieties of annuities and while they can provide highly conservative growth with minimal risk if from an upright company, the amount you invest initially and your monthly contributions can be reduced substantially by the high commission the broker or advisor takes.

Allow me to repeat myself: Regardless of what type of account you have, if you are willing to spend at least a few hours once a month or better yet 20 minutes a week to oversee your investments, they will be more secure and grow substantially larger.

The Value of Lifestyle Funds or ETFs for Safe Investing

A lifestyle fund is an investment strategy that features a mix of funds or ETFs determined by the level of risk and return that is appropriate for an individual investor, usually based upon age. Factors that determine this mix include an investor's age, level of risk aversion, the investment's purpose, and when you expect to retire. This philosophy basically revolves around the concept that when you are young you can take more risks with your money than when you are older.

If you use Lifestyle funds/ETFs they are designed to be the main investment in your portfolio. The purpose of a lifestyle fund may be defeated if other funds are chosen at the same time because the asset allocation ratio will become distorted.

There are a number of ways this allocation can work, but here are a few simple examples:

Age Inv	US Stocks	Foreign Stocks	Bonds
20 – 39	60%	20%	20%
40 – 50	50%	20%	30%
51 – 65	40%	15%	45%
66+	20%	10%	70%

As you can see from the progression, you put your money into more stable and conservative choices as you get older, reducing your risk. Even the choices of stocks should become more stable. For example, from stocks with high-gain potential to stocks with some gain potential that also issue dividends.

Lifestyle funds are offered by different brokers and the funds are typically named to indicate when they expire or you retire such as Lifestyle 2025 or Lifestyle 2050. If you want to be an aggressive investor but don't want to watch the market all the time, you could invest in a lifestyle fund designed for many years until retirement such as 2050 and then every five years switch again to one that is the most years away. On the other hand if you want to play it super conservative you would pick a lifestyle investment that is only five years away. Realize though the drawbacks of Lifestyle funds/ETFs – they are set up for the "average" person, not specifically for you.

Thrift Savings Plan

There is another type of investment limited to government employees. The Thrift Savings Plan (TSP) is one of three components of the Federal Employees Retirement System (FERS) for employees within the United States civil service.

A defined contribution plan, the TSP was established by Congress in 1986 and offers the same types of savings and tax benefits that many private corporations offer their employees under 401(k) plans. In other words, the retirement income received from a TSP account will depend on how much you—and your agency, if you are eligible to receive agency contributions—put into your account during your working years and the earnings accumulated over that time. TSP is a unique retirement plan and a major benefit to those who enroll and use it wisely to manage the retirement account and secure their future.

While some may consider its simplicity a disadvantage, for the average person it makes handling their retirement very easy.

The challenge with the TSP is that it uses just five key proprietary funds so you can't invest in your favorite company no matter how much you like Apple or Disney or

Ford or any other of the thousands of companies. You cannot even invest in just energy or retail mutual funds. But on the other hand, you don't have to evaluate dozens of funds or ETFs or thousands of stocks.

The TSP G Fund is the default fund where the government deposits your automatic contributions. It is ultra conservative, basically matching inflation so the value of the money remains constant. Unless you move your money out of the G Fund it will not grow. Again, this is an ultra-conservative bond fund designed to match inflation. While you may not be losing money you will not be building a retirement account that will support you in your retirement years either.

The other four funds are:

- F Fund is also a bond type fund but with greater gains than the G Fund so your money will grow slightly.

- C Fund is designed to match the core of the S&P 500 market index of the largest companies in this group of 500 companies.

- S Fund tries to emulate the largest U.S. companies that comprise the Dow Jones. The S Fund almost always produces greater gains than the C Fund.

- I Fund represents a group of foreign funds.

The C, S, and I Funds all represent their respective markets as a whole and not any particular segments or individual stocks, which makes these funds more volatile than the G or F funds so they can swing between major gains to major losses.

There are additional lifetime funds, L Funds, which change their assortment between the five primary funds based upon when you retire. The catch with these funds is similar to regular Lifestyle funds as the government administrators presume that everyone is alike and will have the exact same financial needs, goals, and challenges during both their investment years and in retirement.

The individual funds of the TSP retirement account are not traded on any public stock market, which makes it difficult to develop a strategy to track and measure returns. While an investment software cannot use the government TSP funds to analyze and make decisions because the government doesn't release the day-to-day data, there are a few mutual funds and ETFs that accurately duplicate the TSP funds. By putting these funds into a program and developing back-tested strategies you can know when to shift your money from one fund to another, or even develop a portfolio with your money split amongst the different funds to give you the best return based on your personal desires.

Implementing a good TSP management plan does require a few cautions and an overall strategy:

> • The TSP trading rule is that only two trades (transfers) can be made each month other than into the G Fund.

> • Use personal investment management software to guide your decision making for

when and where to move your money
amongst the various TSP funds.

Putting your retirement account to work for you will result in providing a sizeable retirement account and less financial stress. This should only take 20 to 30 minutes every few weeks once you have your TSP strategies setup.

Analysis of the various fund returns, as in reports by the TSP administrators, indicates:

• There is rarely a reason to invest in the G Fund as the F Fund surpasses it during most years. The G fund is only slightly better than putting one's money under the mattress.

• Regular payroll deposits should be made into the F Fund and then re-distributed in a future month.

• Strategies based on which TSP fund to use can produce better returns than just leaving the money in one fund forever or even dividing your money amongst the different funds and leaving it so invested forever.

The key for US government employees is not only to participate in the TSP but to actively setup their account, review it either weekly or once a month, and develop a strategy that will provide for the greatest growth with a risk level that you can accept.

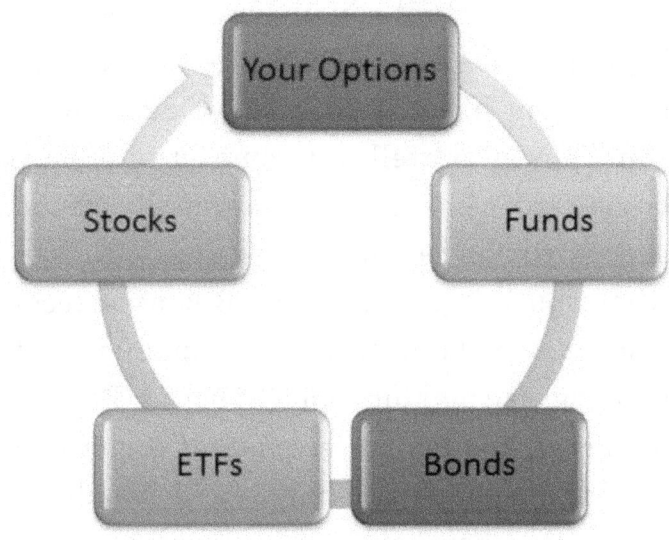

Stocks

By definition, a stock is a share in the ownership of a public company. Buying stock in a company means that you are one of the many owners—or shareholders—and as such, you are entitled to a share of the company's earnings.

Generally speaking, companies issue stock when they want or need to raise money. Instead of borrowing the money from a bank or venture capitalist or issuing bonds—called debt financing—they raise money by selling part of the company: by issuing stock—called equity financing. The first sale of a stock, which is issued by the private company itself, is called the initial public offering (IPO). The advantage of issuing stock is that the company isn't required to pay back the money or make interest payments.

It is important you understand the difference between buying bonds and buying stock. When you buy a debt investment like a bond, you are guaranteed the return of your money as well as promised interest payments. But buying stock has no such guarantees. You simply hope the shares you invest in will someday be worth more than what you bought them for. But as a technical co-owner you take on the risk of the company not being successful and never making any money. If a company goes bankrupt and liquidates, you, as a shareholder, don't get any money until the banks and bondholders have been paid out. Shareholders can earn a lot if a company is successful as the value of it's' shares rises, but they also stand to lose their entire investment if the company isn't.

Some companies pay out dividends, but many others don't, nor is there any obligation to. Without dividends, an investor can only make money on a stock if its shares increase in value.

Investing in stocks also allows you to buy and sell just about any day at any time. However stocks tend to be more susceptible to the ups and downs of the markets and world events. While mutual funds and ETFs are less susceptible to major losses, they are equally less likely to achieve soaring gains.

There is no question stocks carry inherent risk, but they also provide a greater return on your initial investment, a greater opportunity to increase the value of

54

your retirement account—if you are willing to take the risk. Stocks have historically outperformed other investments such as bonds or savings accounts, with an average return of around 10 to 12 percent.

Overcoming Emotions

Today with the Internet, computers, and smartphones it is easy to invest with stocks but it can be scary because it's like putting all your eggs in one basket. If that stock goes down you lose. At least with ETFs and mutual funds there is a level of built-in diversification.

One of the challenges with investing in stocks is controlling your emotions in order to buy and sell what is best for your wallet—not necessarily for your heart. Too often basic human nature prevents us from letting go. Just look at how much stuff is stashed in garages, closets, and basements. The same thing happens when we buy stock in our favorite company and it just kind of muddles along or even goes down, down, down. We don't want to let go and sell it; we hold out believing it will become popular again and go back up. And it may – in two or five or 20 years, but that doesn't help your wallet today.

When investing in stocks it is important to:

- have a non-emotional decision based system
- use professional sources for creating groups of potential stocks
- keep your portfolio manageable
- keep your portfolio diversified

Mutual Funds

Imagine half a dozen investors, sitting at home, each trying to figure out the best way to invest in the stock market. They could each go out and buy a few stocks on their own, but who has the time or resources to manage a portfolio of 50 or 100 stocks? Instead, they decide to band together. They pool all of their money and hire a professional investment manager to invest it for them.

To keep track of who invested what, each investor receives shares, representing their stake in the total investment. Because it's your money, you want to know how much your investment is worth...every day. So every day the manager of this mutual fund tallies up the value of everything it owns and divides it by the number of shares that exist. Whammo-presto: you know exactly what each share is worth. If you want to buy more shares, you know the amount of cash to send the mutual fund manager for each share. If you want to sell shares, you know exactly how much cash to expect in return.

It's an elegant system, and mutual funds have existed for close to 100 years. They currently provide exposure to stocks, bonds, commodities, and other assets.

Investing with mutual funds can be easy if you approach it right. As with anything and everything else in life, you have to make some basic decisions at the beginning to get yourself off on the right foot.

Mutual funds offer two distinct advantages for the investor with limited time. First, each fund is a composite of investments in stocks and so reduces the risk of losses.

Second, each fund has a manager or team of managers that can—and do—switch the fund's investment portfolio around to find the best stocks for the fund.

Any casual glance at investment or money magazines or a search on the Internet will give you a list of mutual fund companies that will all claim to have the best results. But they are not all equal, which you can see by checking publications like *Money* to see which funds and fund families have the best performance.

Investing in mutual funds requires certain key actions:

> • Pick one to three mutual fund families you prefer to work with.
>
> • Create three or four groups of mutual funds so you can pick the best particular one or two funds from each group in which to place your money.
>
> • Decide how frequently you are willing to trade to change your investment portfolio.

These three steps require some time for research on your part, or you can go with recommendations that can be found in magazines like *Kiplinger's* and *Money* magazine. They can also be found in some software packages that have tested various funds and groups of funds.

There are other factors involved in picking mutual funds once you have decided on the primary families you want to work with.

The class of the fund. Typically, fund companies create classes for the fund. The most popular class is *no load,* meaning there is no trading fee to either buy or sell the fund. But other classes charge commissions to buy or to sell or both. These commissions can be steep and are taken right off the top of your investment dollars. There is a ticker symbol for each class, so be careful what symbol you pick.

Holding requirements. Most companies require that you hold a fund a minimum number of days before you sell it. While they may permit you to sell before the hold period is up, the fund family will charge you a short-term trading fee (or penalty) to do so. In the case of a crashing market as we experienced at the beginning of the recent Great Recession, it may be worth it to pay the penalty. The hold times can vary by family and by individual funds but are typically 30, 60, or 90 days.

In and out trading. Also called round-trip, is when you sell a fund and then buy it back. Mutual fund companies don't like that and if you do it too often—usually four such trade pairs within 12 months—they will freeze your portfolio or even cancel your account. In other words, frequent trading in most mutual funds requires careful action. The exceptions are Rydex Funds and ProFunds; but these still have their unique characteristics.

Diversity. A group of mutual funds should not consist of all the same exact type, energy for example, because then all you will be picking is one or another of the same.

Instead, create groups based on sectors, for example: domestic, foreign, strong dividends, etc.

Once you have selected the type of groups, fund families, and actual funds in your groups, or taken recommendations, you are ready to work with these and start investing your money.

Benefits of Mutual Fund Investing

Mutual fund investing is a primary way of building a retirement portfolio and also an easy way for you to invest in the stock market. Many 401k accounts work solely with mutual funds. Investing in mutual funds can provide you with three key benefits:

Management. Each fund has a manager. This manager generally studies the particular industry of the fund and watches all the potential stocks that the fund could buy or does own. The manager trades stocks within the fund to try and produce the greatest return with the most stability. In effect a fund manager is a portfolio manager for a portion of your account.

Diversification. Since a fund holds many stock positions, the risk factor of losing your money is less. If one stock held by the fund goes down, that loss is offset by the others continuing to be stable or gaining in value. Of course if the particular industry covered by the fund is suffering then the value of the mutual fund itself will also decline.

Ease of investing. Because mutual funds trade based on each day's closing prices—except for a few fund families—they are less susceptible to major daily price swings, you don't need to be an intra-day or even a day trader to invest in mutual funds. You can easily manage your retirement account by just examining your portfolio of mutual funds once a week or even just monthly.

Successful use of mutual funds still requires some common sense and time. Just buying a few highly rated funds through a broker's screener software doesn't mean you can then stick your head in the sand and become a millionaire when you pull your head out 10 or 20 years later. Too many retirement accounts lost 40–60 percent of their value during the 2007-2009 Great Recession.

Even when using mutual funds, it is best to diversify and hold a number of funds—anywhere from four to eight would help provide a good mix. There are mutual funds that cover just about any type of investment category whether it be a specific industry like energy or a type of company like large vs. small. There are also funds comprised of stocks known for issuing dividends and funds comprised of different type bonds that issue regular payments.

For example, a portfolio based on mutual funds could contain:

- foreign fund, i.e. Latin America
- large cap fund
- small cap fund
- energy fund
- consumables fund

- high-yield dividend fund
- mid-term government bond fund

Remember, one thing to be careful of in putting together a portfolio based on mutual funds is to not duplicate. Don't pick similar funds from different mutual fund families. This not only reduces your diversification and extends your risk factor but also limits your potential for profit.

Selecting and monitoring mutual funds can be accomplished easily by using:

- your broker's online screener;

- an investment software program that not only helps you pick funds based on performance but also signals when to sell them; and

- magazine articles and issues that rate and categorize funds. Just remember that such articles are usually based on information that is anywhere from one to four weeks old.

As noted previously, most mutual funds have restrictions on how frequently you can trade without paying a penalty. Many fund families also have what is called round-trip penalties. These penalties literally stop you from making any type of trade for a year if you violate the fund's rules which typically say you can't sell and buy back any combination of the same funds four times in a year.

The drawback to investing solely in mutual funds is that you may be at greater risk of losing your money during a major or long-term drop in the markets like our recent recession. This is precisely why during this recession you heard about so many people losing more than 50 percent in the value of their retirement account.

ETFs

Exchange-traded funds (ETFs) are a kind of cross-breed between mutual funds and individual stocks. ETFs have been around since 1993, but they became extremely popular in recent years because they don't have the fees and holding requirements of funds and can be traded at any time like stocks.

ETFs can invest in stocks, bonds, commodities, currencies, or a blend of assets. ETF shareholders are entitled to a proportion of the profits, such as earned interest or dividends paid, and they may get a residual value should the fund be liquidated. Shareholders do not directly own or have any direct claim to the underlying investments in the fund; rather they indirectly own these assets.

As an exchange-traded fund, you buy shares in an ETF directly from any brokerage account. Just like you buy shares in a stock, you can buy through your Schwab or Fidelity account and buy any ETF you want. You can also do it *whenever* you want. While orders to buy or sell a traditional mutual fund are processed only once per day, ETF trades can take place any time the market is open. You can buy shares in the morning and sell them in the afternoon if you so desire.

As when choosing stocks or mutual funds, selecting an ETF-based plan requires a bit of research. Check out the performance for not just the last year but for a number of years. This will give you an idea of how the manager does in producing performance at different times.

Some people think of an ETF as a form of index fund because its goal is to provide investors with a benchmark return at minimal cost. Index funds are mutual funds designed to track the returns of a market index. The first index fund was established in 1976 by John C. Bogle, the founder of investment company Vanguard. Believing it was more important to stay invested than to constantly trade in then out, he created a fund—the Vanguard 500—that tracked the S&P 500. Today there are hundreds of index ETFs, each tracking their own benchmark at a fraction of active management fees.

If ETFs interest you and you are not sure which ones to choose, you can use an investment software program to help select and then monitor their performance. In this way you can easily compare one to another and be sure you are in the right ones that meet your objective.

Stocks, ETFs or Funds?

Whether you choose stocks, mutual funds, or ETFs depends primarily on your willingness to accept the risk of losing, your available time to manage your investments, and the profits you are looking to achieve. However, where you choose to invest doesn't have to be exclusive to just one type or another; you can mix and match. Each of these basic investment types has their own pluses and minuses.

Investing in stocks allows you to pick individual companies such as Ford or Apple. In buying stocks you are banking on the company to prosper so that its shares increase in value, growing your account. With the right pick the potential for a major profit is great. On the other hand, the potential for a major loss is equally great should the company falter, the economy tanks, or world events scare investors.

Mutual funds offer some protection from the potential traumatic rollercoaster effects that can occur with individual stocks because these funds are composed of many stocks based upon the nature or description of the fund. A utility fund, for example, could consist of stocks from electric companies, natural gas companies, and telephone companies.

As I mentioned, each fund is managed, meaning the manager of the fund will buy and sell individual stocks to produce the best returns for the fund as a whole. Since the fund is invested in many stocks, it lessens the overall impact should one of the stocks nosedive. It's the investment example of strength in numbers to help protect your money while still offering growth.

The buying and selling of mutual funds is governed by many more rules than either stocks or ETFs.

ETFs are similar to mutual funds but are not managed on a daily basis because once an ETF is built with the various company stocks it tends to remain with those holdings. In this respect an investor buying ETFs is still diversifying his holdings when he buys a utility ETF.

An advantage of ETFs over mutual funds is that they trade like stocks. This means you can buy and sell at any time. There are no minimum hold times.

In terms of risk and greatest potential profits these three types of investments would rank: stocks, ETFs, mutual funds. In terms of time requirements, you can invest in any of the three regardless of whether you have lots of time or very little. However, if you have less than an hour a month, stocks would be more risky unless you are buying strictly for the long term such as blue chip stocks.

CHAPTER 6: TRADING STRATEGY

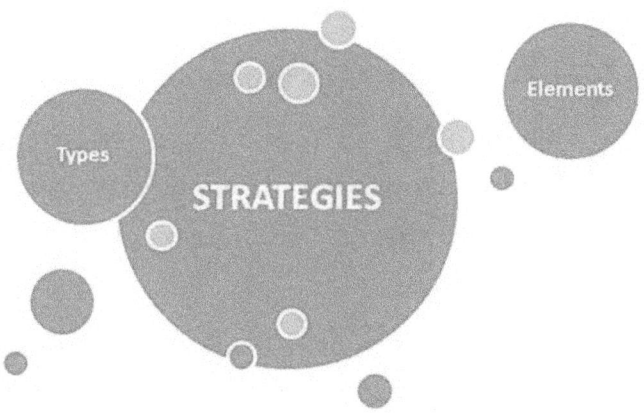

A strategy is like a roadmap that guides you from home to your next destination; without it you could get lost or waste your time and money. Investing requires a strategy or a series of trading strategies.

There are principles to be followed in setting up your investment portfolios. I suggest that each portfolio have about eight investment positions of stocks or mutual funds or ETFs. The key principal here is that each investment position is best derived from an individual strategy, and most likely the strategy is unique to that investment. In other words, one shoe does not fit all your strategies.

Let me give you a few examples. Suppose out of eight investments one is based on a group of foreign ETFs and another is based on a group of Fidelity's select mutual funds. Each group will result in one investment choice and each group will have a different strategy because the ticker symbols in each group are unique and move differently. Yes, you can use the same buy/sell rules for each strategy but you will not come close to maximizing your potential profit.

Identifying Your Investment Strategy

Determining whether you want a conservative investment strategy or a moderate investment strategy depends on a number of factors, such as your personality and your goals.

> • What kind of risk are you willing to accept? A few losses will always occur but are you willing to accept only minor losses or do you want to shoot for large gains that may result in more losses in the process?

> • How often do you want to trade? Are you willing to trade each week or would you prefer only once or twice a month or even less?

> • Are you willing to see your portfolio, your retirement account, or wealth account build very gradually over time or do you want to grow these fast?

Next, it's important to understand the strategy ingredients that make for conservative, moderate, or aggressive investments. For example:

> • Frequent trading, almost daily, is best suited for aggressive, and in some cases, moderate investments.

• Trading a wide range of stocks versus ETFs or many mutual funds will generally produce more aggressive or moderate investment strategies.

Setting different rules or parameters in your retirement software or personal investment software can affect your results and define your investment strategy as either conservative, moderate, or aggressive:

Ranking. Setting sell rules based on the rank of a position (ticker symbol) in your group of potential positions. Ranking in the top 5 percent or 10 percent vs. the top 30 percent will produce more frequent trading and normally a more aggressive strategy.

Stops. Setting the sell rules based on how much a position drops from its high point can also result in trading frequency, churning of your portfolio; if the stops are too low (say 1% or 2%).

Hold rules. Defining your strategy by saying you prefer to hold positions for no less than 10 days vs. 30 or 60 days sets up your strategy for aggressive vs. conservative.

Employing a market exit signal based on the equity curve of the stock markets' performance can tell you when to pause or even cash out for a short or long time and by doing so preserve your money from losses. But setting this signal with a short evaluation period versus a long period can have consequences: set it too long and you won't get a signal in time to avert major loss, but set it too short and you will trade too frequently.

Period of analysis. When you are analyzing your group of potential funds, ETFs, or stocks, the time period selected will also determine the type of investment strategy. Longer analysis periods will result in more conservative approaches while short periods, like 10 days, will be more aggressive and require more trading.

All these factors are not as intimidating as they may sound. The key to defining your investment strategy is understanding that you are in control and can set these parameters to meet your personality and objectives. Tailor the analysis testing in your investment software to fall within your range of what is acceptable to you.

Why Having Just One Strategy Doesn't Work

Having a sole buy/sell strategy sounds great in theory but safe investing requires more than putting all your eggs in one basket.

Different groups react differently to analysis. Stocks, for example, have different price movement characteristics from mutual funds and ETFs. Mutual funds and ETFs are composites of stocks, so their momentum or even moving average is generally different from any particular stock. Mutual funds also are different from ETFs because they are a managed group of tickers that can—and do—change in contrast to ETFs, which are more set in their composition.

Furthermore, once you have a strategy of signals developed for a particular universe, changing that universe (group) changes its dynamics because adding a new ticker most likely has a different momentum or moving average than the group as a whole. This means any change to a group requires new back-testing or optimization to find the best potential returns based on your investing goals.

Different types of analysis may work best for different types of groups. After extensive research and testing, for example, I found that in general ETFs usually give the best results when analyzed with the *relative strength momentum formula* while funds provide the best results when analyzed with the *alpha formula*.

In *Technical Analysis of the Financial Markets*, John J. Murphy explains that market momentum "is measured by continually taking price differences for a fixed time interval. To construct a 10-day momentum line, simply subtract the closing price 10 days ago from the last closing price." Put another way, momentum measures the rate of the rise or fall in stock prices. Michael Carr, in his book *Safe Profitable Investing with Relative Strength,* explains the differences between seven types of relative strength analysis.

Most mutual fund investments are for mid- to long-term periods of a few months to years while stocks may be used for weeks, months, or years, and the same is true for ETFs.

Developing a successful long-term strategy requires careful back-testing based on your objectives and basic parameters. For example you may never want to hold a position if it drops more than 9 percent from a high, so in setting your test you would set 9 percent as the maximum stop you would allow.

Once you establish your guidelines, you can run a back-testing optimization with your investment software. Prove to yourself how changing just one element of a strategy can affect the result by changing a setting. With anywhere from three to eight parameters in a strategy you can see how making one change can have dramatic effects. Another self-test would be to take a strategy you like and add or subtract a ticker from the group to see how the results are affected.

Developing strategies that meet your goals for each group or universe of symbols is the homework part of investing safely for the long-term. Once you have your strategies they rarely require change and future optimizations need only be done every few years

Why You Need a Conservative Strategy

I would suggest your goal is to build a portfolio of investments with different positions based upon different strategies. Regardless of what type investor you are you should invest some of your money conservatively. If you follow the principle of diversification, whether you are a conservative or aggressive investor, there is always room for profitable investing that minimizes risk. This is especially important for a retirement focused portfolio.

Talking about a conservative strategy doesn't mean all your investments must be conservative. If you are diversifying your money with seven or eight stocks, or ETFs, or mutual funds, then one of these can surely be a conservative investment.

There are three main types of conservative strategies.

Bonds. Create a group of 7–15 bond funds or ETFs, each slightly different from the other so you have choices from which to pick, such as corporate bonds versus government or long-term versus short-term. With a group like this you can shift your money from one type to another depending upon the economy to take advantage of whichever is producing the best return.

The drawback to using bond mutual funds is that the fund families usually place restrictions that require you to hold the funds for 60–90 days. Bond ETFs trade like stocks and so have no trading restrictions.

When using bonds be sure not to duplicate. In other words don't have a short-term government bond from both Fidelity and another from Vanguard because when analyzing and making buy/sell decisions you could end up just moving from one to another of the same type when you should be moving to a totally different type (i.e. going from short-term to long-term).

High dividend stocks. Generally speaking, stocks that pay high dividends are relatively stable while growing at a slow but steady rate. These stocks pay dividends, which is similar to earning interest on your money in a savings account, at rates of 4–8 percent annually.

Again, you can put together a watch group of these stocks. Find them by searching the Standard & Poor website, via Morningstar, or your broker's website.

Remember that when investing in these type stocks you only reap the benefits of the dividend payouts if you hold them mid- to long-term. If you trade frequently you will miss out on getting the dividends unless you just luck out. If you invest in ETFs or mutual funds based on high-dividend stocks you have a better chance of reaping the interest payments.

Basic ETF indexes. You can create a small watch group of three to five ETFs to follow for safe profitable investing. Such a group will enable you to move from one conservative position to another. One group that I have used contains:

- SPY–SST Spider 500, which emulates the S&P 500
- IEF–iShares 7–10 year Treasury bond
- MINT–PIMCO enhanced short maturity

I compare the performance of these against the S&P 500 itself to gauge which is doing the best and where to put my money.

By using one of these investment types in your portfolio you can minimize risk and have a fallback strategy for when the markets go south and you want to move your other monies out of more aggressive strategies into a safer position until the markets start to surge again.

Smart Strategies for Conservative Investors

Almost everyone is a conservative investor to some degree but if you are always concerned about not losing your hard-earned cash, then you probably fit the mold for a true conservative investor. The good news is that there are sound strategies for conservative investors that can still grow your money—maybe not like a bamboo tree but surely like a solid oak tree.

And there is nothing wrong with saying you are a conservative investor, that you want to leave the risky stock investing to others. When retirement comes, or a rainy day, conservative investors are confident they will have money to meet their future needs.

There are degrees of conservative investing.

- **First**: totally concerned and committed to just about not risking a penny of your cash but desiring to at least keep even with inflation
- **Second**: committed to minimal risk of your money but desiring to see it grow a little more than inflation
- **Third**: conservative in most cases but willing to use a small portion of your cash to grow faster than inflation but not to the extent of taking wild risks

If you fall in the first category, safe investments can be found in:

- bonds, bond ETFs, or bond mutual funds
- some stocks (companies) with a 10-year or longer history of paying strong dividends, ETFs, or mutual funds based on dividend paying stocks
- US treasuries, ETFs, or mutual funds based on treasuries

If you fit the profile for the second category you should invest similarly to those in the first category but put more of your funds into dividend paying stocks, funds, or ETFs. This will enable your portfolio to grow a bit more than inflation as dividend payouts from strong companies are usually greater than inflation and there is also a good likelihood the price of the stock, ETF, or fund is also appreciating.

For those of you in the last category of basically conservative investors, the majority of your portfolio should be invested as if you were in the first category. And like those in category #2 you should hold investments in dividend paying stocks, funds, or ETFs to help grow your portfolio and beat inflation. But this portion of your portfolio should be a strong minority.

Also, if you're a #3, you should invest directly in stocks, ETFs, or mutual funds based primarily on large companies—called large caps—strong, stable companies whose growth may be slow but sure. Another option is to take a small minority of your money and invest in ETFs or mutual fund sectors representing those portions of the economy that are growing.

Just because your investments are conservative doesn't mean that once you buy them you should hold on forever. Situations change and you may need to make adjustments. For example, you may want to switch from long-term bonds to short- or mid-term bonds. Or maybe one of your dividend-paying stocks is at 3.5 percent but there is another paying 4.7 percent.

In all situations, it is still important for all conservative investors to keep on top of the market to some degree. You don't have to watch it daily, but taking a glance every week or for sure every three or four weeks is a good idea.

Mutual Fund Investment Strategies

In developing mutual fund strategies for your retirement account it is important to recognize that most software programs, especially chart-based programs, are designed to work best with stocks or ETFs. The holding requirements, short-term trading fees, and round-trip penalties of most mutual fund companies require different software programs.

Whoa, let's stop a moment and review what I just said about funds (in case you missed this earlier):

> • *Holding requirements & short-term trading fees*. Most fund families don't like you to trade too often and they place restrictions on the funds. For example they may say that 'fund A' must be held 60 days or you will pay a penalty of 2% if you sell it early.

• ***Round-trip penalties***. Just like most fund families don't like you to trade too frequently they also don't want you going back and forth buying and selling the same fund. Usually if you do more than four roundtrips within 12 months involving different funds they may lock your account for a year so you can't trade at all; or in a worst case scenario, cancel your account.

You should ultimately have about eight investment positions. For example, you could place all your positions in Fidelity Select funds, but this would be like betting on just the Eastern Division of baseball's American League for the best teams in all of major league baseball. The result will not be nearly as good or as safe as if you had three or four other groups of mutual funds.

My sources for mutual fund groups include:

- Fidelity
- Vanguard
- *Money* magazine's list of best performing funds

There are thousands of mutual funds available—thousands. But you only need groups with as few as ten—at the most one hundred funds—in order to give you good investment choices.

In addition to the groups based on their source, you can create groups based on class or industry by going to any of the broker sites or magazines listed above then filtering with these criteria as an example:

- bonds for a constant conservative investment
- dividends for a constant, possibly conservative, cash flow of 3 percent–8 percent.
- domestic to find the best of what's happening in the US
- foreign to invest in the best or emerging oversea markets

The next step is to either use software that enables you to find the best future performers within each group or perform fundamental analysis such as studying the track record of the manager and his longevity managing the fund. The method I use is the technical analysis of the fund's performance as compared to the markets as a whole. You also need rules for when to sell and when to hold, because failing to sell when you should is what creates losses in your pocketbook.

Let me repeat myself, Technical Analysis removes all emotional and subjective aspects of your decisions. This method can be based on many means of analyzing a fund's price performance. You can do it with a spreadsheet if you have lots of time or with a software program. Programs will tell you what fund is most likely the best performer and also indicate if your current holdings are continuing to grow.

But you have to remember those special mutual fund factors: minimum holding requirements once you buy a fund; short-term penalty fees if you sell too soon, and a possible frozen account if you re-buy a recently sold fund or funds too soon within 12 months. In other words either you or your software must track or base your selling and buying decisions upon how long you have owned a fund with a re-buy restriction on recently sold funds so you don't get caught in the round-trip trap.

One way around the round-trip trap: instead of buying the same fund back, buy a similar fund from a different mutual fund family. In other words switch from company ABC to company XYZ.

Remember: the trading strategy for each group in your retirement account will be different. One group may only require a minimum hold of 30 days while another may require 90 days. A dividend group may result in very infrequent trades while a sector group may trade more frequently because of changes in the economy and offer opportunities for large profits. You may, as I do, have two or even three different strategies for the same group of funds, one based on more frequent trading than the other.

The key is to form your groups, settle on a strategy method for making your buy/sell decisions, and then stick with it.

Picking Your Investments

There are four primary techniques to pick your investments. While you may think you can mingle them, selecting one method to choose your investments works best.

Technical analysis is my preferred strategy because it eliminates or reduces emotion-based decisions and requires minimal time, just 20–60 minutes a week. (I only spend about 15 minutes a week with my software program.) Technical analysis involves analyzing the price movement of a ticker symbol to forecast its future. It works just as well with mutual funds, stocks, and ETFs. When used with rules or parameters to decide when to sell, the potential profit gains can be both quick and substantial. This method can be used for short-term investments of just months or long-term investing where a position is held for many years.

Fundamental analysis involves looking into a company's management, evaluating its profit and loss statements and balance sheets, and reading research reports. This is the method used by famed investor Warren Buffett. Fundamental analysis can take anywhere from weeks to months of evaluation before a buy decision can be reached. This strategy is best suited for those with lots of time and for those investing for the long, long-term with no need to see substantial gains in months or even a few years.

Newsletter subscription means you will take the advice of someone else, a newsletter writer who makes buy-or-sell recommendations. There are hundreds of investment newsletters. There are conservative and aggressive newsletters; there are pessimistic ones (bears) always predicting a market decline and optimistic ones (bulls) always saying the market will be going up.

Every newsletter writer will tell you they predicted this or that and with their suggestions you would have reaped enormous gains. They all say this even though they almost all disagree on what to buy.

I know a writer who claims he predicted the market crash of the Great Recession. The catch is that he predicted it every month or every other month for five years. If you had taken his advice you would have totally missed the bull market that preceded the recession.

Personal choice is the other method of choosing your investments. In reality it should be called emotional choice. Many years ago I decided to buy Northwest Airlines. Why? Because I had flown more trips on Northwest than any other airline and read good comments about them in the *Wall Street Journal*. And when I sold my shares I made a decent profit. But a few years later I decided that since I profited from them once before I should buy them again. This time though I lost money and my loss was greater than my original gain. That is emotional buying.

Emotional buying can be based on tips, your friend's advice, your kid's favorite toy, or just because you had a good time at the movies. I don't recommend buying on an emotional, personal choice basis. It is gambling and while there are winners in gambling it is the casinos that make the most money.

Hiring a financial planner or registered investment advisor (RIA). By hiring a professional you are asking someone else to manage your money and giving up almost all control over your investments. If you have zero time to manage your investments, your 401k, or your IRA retirement account, then this is a good way to go.

Since you are hiring someone, it means you are the boss. So just like at any other employer you should look over the candidates' résumés, their past performance, and interview them to see if they fit with your goals and objectives.

- Where will they invest your money: stocks, ETFs, or mutual funds?
- Can he work with your goals and objectives?
- Are they registered or certified?
- How did most of their clients actually fare during the last recession?
- How do they earn their money? Are they fee based, taking a percentage of the value of the portfolio—which I think is the best way—or do they take a commission on each trade and if so how much?

Interviewing financial planners or investment advisors is critical. Just like some men have brown hair and others gray, advisors can be divided into various camps: conservative, aggressive, or moderate. They may have their own investment programs or maybe they only invest in mutual funds or long-term investment strategies. In other words, their investment philosophy is important because it will have a direct bearing on your retirement account.

If you decide to hire a professional to manage your money then you must let them do it and not micromanage. You have to let the advisor do the job once you hired them. Yes, you want reports and some communication but an employee can't do their job if you stand over their shoulder all the time.

If you have zero time, not even 30 minutes a month, you should hire a professional to manage your retirement rather than just occasionally looking at your account or neglecting it altogether. It is best to pay someone 1 percent or so to help grow your money than just leaving to chance.

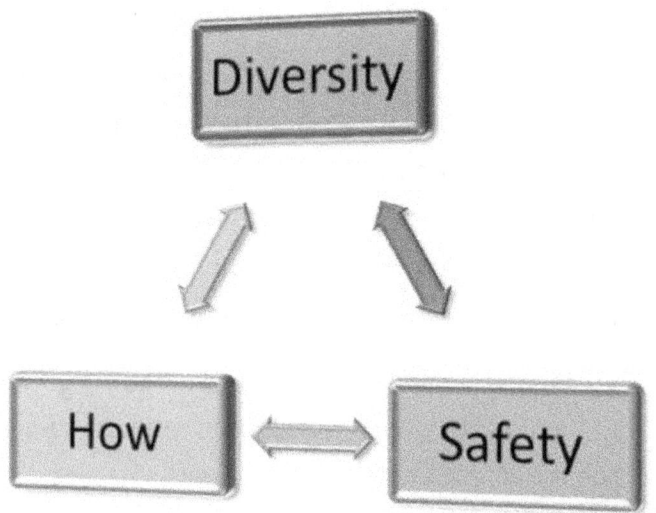

Diversifying your portfolio is kind of like blending coffee beans to create the best cup of coffee that will be unique to you. You may, for example, want to develop a portfolio based on energy, consumer goods, South America, and health.

I happen to be a Pepsi person, but I also enjoy a nice frothy root beer or cream soda from time to time. The point is that I blend my tastes to more than my top preference. The same applies to diversifying or blending your portfolio.

A portfolio that is focused strictly on your comfort zone may result in missed opportunities or suffer unnecessarily during market declines. Adding a few other complementary areas creates more diversification, more opportunities, and less potential risk. Blending some peripheral groups into your portfolio enables you to reallocate your money when one sector of the economy is surging.

Your retirement portfolio represents your likes and dislikes. While you cannot eliminate emotions from investing you can control them so that your diversification goals and investment choices are also based on sound analytics. Combining your emotional personality and analytics dramatically increases the likelihood of success.

Moving a little out of your comfort zone, although not too far, may give you opportunities you would not have otherwise considered.

Primary Keys to Diversification

Diversification based on your age is often cited as critical, yet a good investment plan should be based on a number of the following factors, not just how old you are.

Term refers to how long you expect to hold a particular stock, ETF, or fund—long-term, short-term, or mid-term. If you are going to trade daily then long-term positions are not very likely. On the other hand, if you only want to trade occasionally or monthly then most of your positions will generally be mid-term or long-term.

Type refers to the kind of investment such as stocks, ETFs, or mutual funds. Mutual Funds offer diversification by their very nature as each fund is composed of many individual stocks of the same type or objective (such as utilities or large corporations). This diversification means this type of investment is not as dependent on any one company for success.

Safety. Balancing risk is a key component to diversifying your investments. You can do this by creating different groups to invest in, such as:

- high dividend paying
- US companies
- foreign companies
- bonds
- select type funds
- industry sectors
- asset strength

By investing in six to eight different groups or types of investments it is easy to achieve diversification and still have your portfolio easily manageable. The groups can be all ETFs, for example, or a mix of stocks, ETFs, and mutual fund groups. If you are using a mix of the three types of investments it is important that each one is unique; in other words don't have an energy ETF group and an energy fund group.

My typical categories are:

1. General stock group
2. ETFs – USA domestic
3. ETFs – sectors
4. ETFs – foreign
5. ETFs – basic three or bonds
6. Fidelity Select mutual funds

While there are no precise rules for creating a universe of stocks, a group that is too large becomes unwieldy and makes it more difficult to analyze and find the rising stars. I try to keep my groups under 130 with the majority ranging between 40 and 70 symbols and a few ranging between 12 and 15 symbols.

An important aspect in creating a group is to remember the purpose is *not* to find a winning position but to find potential winners or in some cases to simply group together opposites that my rise and fall as the economy or events dictate. With a diversity of groups you will be in a position to invest in the best performers.

However, just because I have six to eight groups, does not mean I always use them. I would suggest watching these many groups, and if signals are good then, yes, invest in each group. But if, for example, foreign markets are in turmoil and declining, don't invest there. There is nothing wrong with switching your money to a savings account or money market when there are no good buys. It is better to preserve you money than risk it when market conditions are in turmoil. In fact, a few programs like Dynamic Investor Pro will actually signal you when to move to cash, if you set the program up to do so.

Diversify Your Accounts

The main reason to diversify your portfolio is to protect your investments. Most people trade either in their regular account to grow their wealth and cash or in a retirement account. I suggest you ultimately consider three or four accounts such as:

> • Retirement to take care of your later years
> with tax free income

• Wealth to give you more spending cash or for special objectives like a new home or a trip to Italy
• An emergency fund for the unexpected

I know it is difficult enough to manage one account, and for most of us to even come up with the cash to start just one is a challenge. But the benefit of having these three or four different investment accounts is nothing short of spectacular.   When we purchased our home I wanted to improve it pretty much right off the bat. That meant installing the dreamed-about hot tub underneath the canopy of an all cedar gazebo and a few rows of upright juniper trees. I was able to use our personal wealth account without touching the retirement or emergency accounts.

If you need to start one account at a time, start with the retirement account, then the emergency, and finally the wealth and special desire accounts.

Divide and Conquer a 401k

A typical 401k, or other employer offered retirement account includes a wide range of mutual funds, perhaps ETFs and maybe even the companies own stock. The creators of the 401k are trying to give you choices as to where to invest your money; not answers, just choices.

This is where divide & conquer comes in.

Typically your 401k retirement group will contain significant categories of funds: bonds, sectors, asset classes, foreign, and most likely the new "lifestyle" type funds that are a composite of other funds or stocks with dates as part of their name.

By dividing the overall retirement group into three or four sub-groups you will conquer each and develop both safer and more profitable investing strategies.

Typically you can divide your group:

1. Bonds & government treasuries – for more secure investing. But these will produce very low gains, barely keeping up with inflation.

2. Lifestyle funds or ETFs – these are a composite of others funds/ETFs and end with a year number aimed at your potential year of retirement. The further off the year is (i.e. 2055) the more aggressive the fund. They become more conservative as time goes.

3. Sector and asset type funds or ETFs. This will be your primary investment category unless you want to play it very conservative and place most of your money in the bond category, or you simply want to let a fund manager take over – in which case you would put your money in a lifestyle fund.

4. Foreign funds or ETFs may be placed in a separate group, especially if there is a large number available.

With these groups you will be better positioned to succeed and reach your own investment goals.

- Use the bond groups for a small portion of your money so you always have that set aside. You can increase the percentage of your portfolio as time goes on if want to play it extra safe as you near or enter retirement.

- Use the primary group with an investment program to maximize gains and grow your account while at the same type reducing risk

- The foreign group can allow you to invest in those countries experiencing growth. This will help to diversify your portfolio.

- Use a lifestyle fund for a small portion of your portfolio, again, as a means of diversification. You can switch from one "year" fund to another whenever you want to keep your choice as aggressive or conservative as you desire.

Dividing your 401k retirement investment offerings in this manner will enable you to more effectively control and manage your money. You will be able to conquer what can seem to be a mystery much easier and also more easily reach your retirement goals.

Other Diversification Techniques

There are other ways to diversify that are often overlooked such as through adopting a variety of strategies that can help protect your funds and, even more so, enable you to grow your portfolio during almost every economic situation.

Having two or three different strategies for each type of investment group can keep you ahead of market twists and turns, ups and downs. Knowing when to switch from one strategy to another can be easily accomplished by viewing a performance chart with each of your strategies represented. Not all of your investment strategies, just the ones that focus on the same type investment, such as energy ETFs. Checking this chart every week or two can tell you in a glance which trading strategy to use.

Another method of diversification is to differentiate your strategies based on your buy/sell rules. For example, one strategy could have a market exit signal with a short setting for rapid response to market ups and downs while another could be set for a more moderate response that allows for normal market variations without bumping you in and out of your positions with every turn of the market. Or perhaps one is set for a long-term holding that only reacts to a prolonged market slump.

A third diversification technique is similar to viewing the strategies for a particular group or investment type. This technique involves comparing the overall performance of each investment group or category to see if one group underperforms during a particular market. This is one reason to follow six to eight groups of investments so you can capitalize on those that are performing best at any given time.

Looking at the equity curve of your strategies and groups or a combination chart will take but a few moments and quickly tell you which ones are underperforming.

Remember: the purpose of diversifying is to protect your money, your investments, and particularly your retirement account so it can grow to meet your future needs and desires.

You Can Score Great Gains with Dividend Based Investments

Investing in high-yield, consistent dividend paying stocks, funds, or even ETFs is often suggested as a conservative way to get income into your checking account while providing a strong degree of investment security. But it can also provide great gains and huge profits.

I conducted a variety of tests to show how these investments can pay off quite handsomely and build anyone's portfolio, especially a retirement account.

For my test I put together a group of 43 dividend paying stocks that have consistently paid dividends over many years. I added the S&P 500 index symbol, SPX, as a benchmark against which the performance of the others would be compared. Because I wanted to take advantage of the dividend income I set my sell rules to a preference of holding a position at least 90 days.

The test period began with January 2005 and ended at the end of July 2011, a little over six and a half years. During this period the markets as measured by the S&P 500, gyrated thru many ups and downs including the Great Recession of 2008 and its recovery.

The results vary but in general holding more positions at the same time lessens the total potential gain and money you can make. The gains during that 79-month period ranged from 92 percent to 399 percent; on an annual averaged basis the gains ranged from 11 percent to 28 percent.

Positions	One	Two	Three	Four	Five
Percentage Gain	224-399	216	128-151	149	92
& Compound Annual Average %	15-28	19	13-15	15	11-14

Thus with prudent sell and buy rules—especially rules to protect you when the markets dive—you can earn both dividends and substantial gains with a portfolio that includes investing with a group of high-yield dividend paying stocks, ETFs, or mutual funds.

Turbulance

Investing in a turbulent market can be a real challenge. In fact many investors go to the sidelines and simply wait out the crazy times rather than risk losing their money. But this doesn't have to be the case.

It can be unnerving when markets are bouncing up and down rather than moving steadily upwards with just the occasional dips. But it can also still be very profitable if you follow a few key principals.

First, don't succumb to selling or buying that is not based on hard facts that relate specifically to your investment strategies and to particular ticker symbols.

Second, keep your time frame for managing your portfolio. If you examine your portfolio weekly don't succumb to making mid-week or daily decisions because this requires different strategies than your current ones. In other words you can set yourself up for failure and losing money by switching horse's mid-stream. Remember your retirement account is a long-term investment, something you will rely upon for years, even decades.

If you want to react more frequently to the market then you should develop strategies and concepts that work best with daily trading. You can use the same groups of ticker symbols that you prefer to watch but now your buy/sell rules will be different and designed specifically for up/down markets.

Third, be willing to spend a little more time to expand your analysis. If your weekly method, for example, is to have a program compute and give you recommendations based on technical analysis, perhaps you should look at a few charts to see if they confirm holding or buying particular positions that you are considering. In other words, in turbulent markets exercise a bit more caution on the safety side when making your decisions.

Myself, I like looking at the moving average and full stochastic charts, and sometimes I also look at a relative strength crossover chart.

Fourth, take a more frequent look at an overall exit signal that can tell you when to stop trading.

All of these steps reflect the most important aspect of handling turbulent markets: to prepare and if necessary take decisive action. So be prepared to safeguard your investments; be prepared to buy new positions when the markets decide the roller coaster ride is over and it's time to climb the mountain again; and be prepared to hunt for current investment stars despite the turbulence.

Being prepared can also mean having a list already written identifying the exact ETFs or funds you are going to switch your money into when the markets start doing the rollercoaster thing.

Let's look at market turbulence another way: One recent spring my wife and I went for a drive into Glacier National Park. Gray clouds were hanging low encapsulating the mountains and the only other visitor I saw at the viewing spot along Lake McDonald in Apgar left quickly.

There are days, even weeks when the markets tumble and our investment software gives us sell signal after sell signal and we question the buy signals because, well the markets are going down. Our human emotions start to make us question the validity of our investment strategies.

On that same visit to Glacier National Park my wife and I drove out along Camas road, a rarely used, but nicely paved road that leads to a graveled highway and eventually back to civilization. The views along this road were stunning. Perhaps not what you would expect or what we were looking for, but the snow formations amongst the trees, the young tress pushing up and over the snow where bare fire killed trees stood sentinel were captivating. And of course there were big and small waterfalls and creeks cutting their way to the North Fork of the Flathead River.

The same holds true most any day or week for investing, and for ferreting out the rising stocks like the great hidden views in Glacier.

The critical thing in turbulent or strange market situations revolves around two basics.

First, what is the overlying long term trend of the markets? Real market trends involve more than days, weeks or even a few months. Michael Carr, talks about look backs of 250 trading days (that's a year) in his book "Safe Profitable Investing with Relative Strength." And most trends, especially upward trends last for years. Generally I gauge trends based upon 100 trading days – about 4-5 months.

Yes, parts of Glacier were dismal that day, but other parts were shining in their own way.

Benefits of a Major Stock Market Drop

We know the economy can be hammered by political events and posturing or by sudden financial news. This causes market turbulence, where one day the market is up 155 points and down 95 points the next day, which requires a game plan and stalwart constitution.

No one likes to see the stock market drop, especially a major decline. But there is a secret benefit from a major drop in the markets. If you look at a decline in the markets as the glass is half full the opportunities and benefits can be enormous.

• Shed mediocre positions whether they are ETFs, funds or stocks.

• Check your strategies to see how accurate they were in picking up the last rebound so you will catch this one.

• Prepare and be ready to allocate your cash
to meet your diversification and profit goals.

Once you are out of the market and have moved to cash or bond ETFs you are ready to plan for a successful investment future. In other words, don't just sit on the sidelines and stop watching the markets. Take a little time to look back at the charts of your strategies and compare them to the S&P 500 to determine whether they matched or did better the S&P when the last few rebounds occurred.

Once you have reviewed your strategies and are confident about which ones will improve your retirement account in the future you are ready to review your diversification goals. Look at the total value of your portfolio and divide it by the number of positions you wish to hold in the future. If you are going to diversify with eight investments, divide your cash by eight so you will be prepared to spend that much on each position when it is time.

By taking advantage of a market decline you can be even more prepared than ever to grow your portfolio. It's kind of like taking care of a lawn in spring. You know it is going to rain and then rain some more, but if you watch the weather and catch a dry spell of just one or two days you can get the lawn fertilized so when the rains come back your grasses, individual positions, will benefit the most.

CHAPTER 9: TRADING FREQUENCY

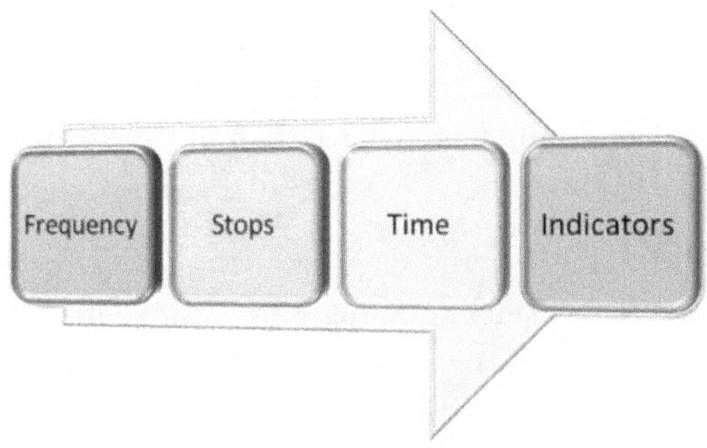

Part of building your portfolio revolves around being ready to act. But this doesn't mean you have to trade every day or even every week if you don't want to. There are numerous rules you can adjust that will allow you to control the frequency of trading. In this way if you only want to look at the market once a week or every few weeks you can do this and still enjoy substantial profits.

Here are the key factors that you can control:

Analysis Period

When analyzing momentum you can set the period of analysis (on a continual basis) for anywhere from five trading days upward. A shorter period of return will react more quickly to market volatility and result in frequent trades whereas if the period of analysis is long, like 90 trading days there will be fewer trades.

Stops

Trailing stops that give a sell signal when a ticker symbol drops from its high can also affect the frequency of trades. If the stop is set at 3 percent there will be substantially more trades than if it is set, for example, at 8 percent,

Hold Time

Some software programs will allow you to specify desired hold times and while they may be overridden by stops or other selling rules, a longer hold time will also reduce the number of trades. For example if you have no hold time then trade signals can occur any time but if you have hold time signals of 30 or 90 days there will be fewer trades unless a stop signal is generated. This is also important if you are investing in mutual funds as it helps to avoid those short-term trading fees.

Chart Settings

How you set the parameters for different charts can equally effective a charts signal to buy or sell. For example, a moving average chart with settings of 10 fast and 50 slow is going to produce more signals than a chart of 20 and 60 or a chart of 50 and 150.

These are but four ways you can control the frequency of trading in your investment portfolio and thus control the amount of time you spend managing your investments. It may be true that gains will not be as robust if you trade very infrequently but that doesn't mean your account will not grow.

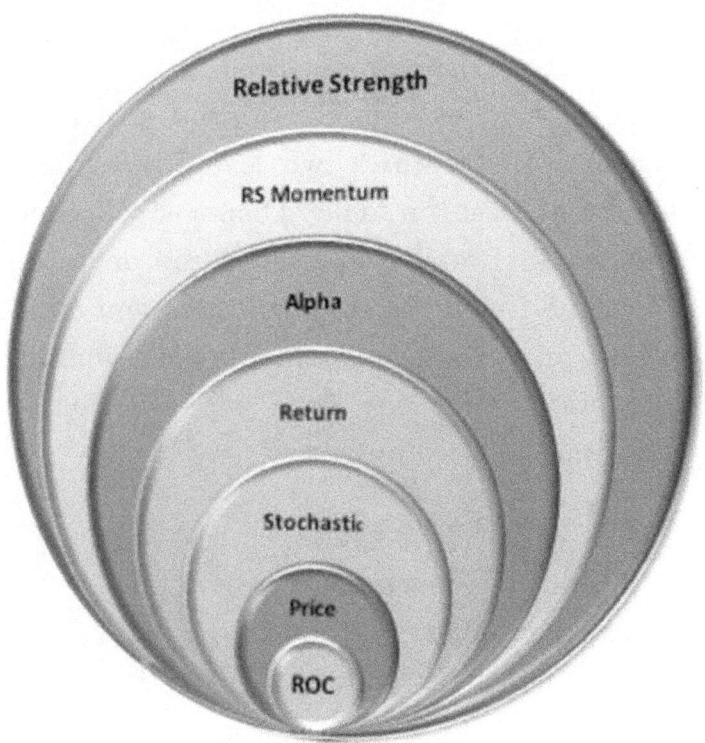

Technical analysis is a method of evaluating securities by analyzing statistics generated by market activity, such as past prices and volume. Technical analysts are not measuring a security's intrinsic value; they use charts and other tools to identify patterns that can *suggest future activity.*

Using technical analysis enables you to change the parameters or rules for when a new buy is suggested. The same analysis with some software programs will tell you when to sell a position based on rules you define or that the program suggests. Using this approach to make investment decisions for your retirement account helps to eliminate human emotion from the process and produce better results.

When we let our emotions get involved in financial matters we risk delaying or even making the wrong decision. Just because we love Disney World is not in itself a good reason to buy Disney stock. Similarly, having a friend in Brazil isn't a good reason to buy the Brazil ETF. And if you already own them you might be tempted to hold on to these investments even when they go down. Our brains may say *sell, sell, sell* but our emotional attachment says otherwise.

Types of Analysis

Using an investment software program based on technical analysis can make the entire buy/sell process easier and more efficient. But there are challenges, including:

- what means of analysis to use
- technical charts
- setting the analysis rules

Before I go into detail let me just mention one thing that many people confuse when discussing technical analysis which is frequently off-handed referred to as "momentum investing"

Momentum investing is simply buying what is going up and selling when it goes down. This is the basis for most charting software, many investment programs and putting your retirement account into this decision arena puts you at great risk. This is like saying I can strike out any batter with a curve ball. *Really?*

There are dozens—if not more—means of analysis, including:

Relative strength (RS) – a broad term covering many types of analysis. RS investing involves calculating the difference of the momentum of, say, an ETF versus other ETFs and the momentum of an index or benchmark like the S&P 500. While a chart can be created for any particular ticker symbol versus the benchmark, the important factor is how each ETF relates to other ETFs, which shows the relative strength of each symbol to others within any particular group or universe of symbols.

It's like comparing horses at the Kentucky Derby. We know that every horse on the track can probably run faster than any other horse in the world so each horse's momentum is greater than my neighbor's quarter horse out on the range. But picking the winner is just like buying based on momentum alone. Yes, they are all winners, but only one is going to be the winner, and only a few are going to bring home any prize money.

On the other hand, relative strength investing says that a particular horse's speed is greater than the average horse and also is greater by a specific amount than every other horse on the track. And if you know the running speeds and durability factors of each horse (or each ticker symbol) you can bet on or buy the most likely winner.

This sounds complicated but there are formulas for calculating relative strength. You can do the calculations yourself in a spreadsheet but the easiest way is to use a software program that performs technical analysis that includes alpha or relative strength momentum.

Return can be defined for both technical analysis and fundamental analysis; yet the definition is different. Return in fundamental analysis is a calculation used to assess a company's efficiency at allocating the capital (money) under its control to profitable operations. Return on invested capital gives a sense of how well a company is using its money to generate profit. By comparing a company's return on capital with its weighted average cost of capital, you can see if the company is using its invested capital effectively.

Return for our technical analysis purposes here is pretty straight forward, which is why it's popular. Return is perhaps the simplest, most basic of relative strength type analysis. It is simply a measure of gains and losses. When it is compared to the benchmark (S&P 500) you are seeing how much greater or less the price progression of a ticker symbol is compared to the price progression of the benchmark. And when you compare all the symbols in a group the ranking is simply which one did better than another against the benchmark. Some refer to return as momentum.

In fact many chart programs are in effect illustrating the return of a ticker symbol simply by showing the movement of the ticker's price. Either it is going up or down or perhaps gyrating nowhere. But normally there is a percentage change almost every day and if you bought and sold on this basis it would be easy to calculate your return just as you can calculate the return from previous days or history.

If you analyze a particular symbol that is part of a group of symbols using return over a particular time period you will quickly see which symbol has outperformed the others. You can take this a step further and say that the symbol with the best return for the past 10 or 30 days out of your group is the one to now buy. Investing in this manner can be very successful as the analysis indicates which symbols have the greatest growth or loss rate.

Relative strength momentum. Now things get a bit more complicated. RSM compares the momentum over whatever set period (trading days) versus the momentum of the benchmark. This is not just return points but a calculation of how great, or not so great, the point movement is over the selected time period. Again, this is compared to the benchmark and then a ranking based upon the comparison to the benchmark.

Alpha is one of the more complicated types of relative strength analysis. It is similar to relative strength momentum (RSM) but alpha goes a step further. Now instead of just comparing the momentum against the benchmark and ranking all the symbols in the group like with RSM, the momentum calculation of each symbol is also compared with the momentum calculation of every other symbol in the group and then a ranking is produced. Generally speaking Alpha is a slightly more aggressive approach to relative strength analysis.

The difference between return and alpha is that alpha is calculating not just the progress of the ticker symbol over your selected time period but it is comparing that progress to a benchmark like the S&P 500 and to all the other symbols in the group. Most importantly, it is factoring in the rate of change and comparing this rate of change between all of the symbols in the group. In other words, alpha is saying symbol X is moving at a more rapid pace than any of the other symbols and its pace also differs from the benchmark more than that of the other symbols in the group.

Price oscillation is the difference of two moving averages in either points or in percentages, so buy and sell signals can be generated as the price oscillator shifts from positive and negative territories.

Moving average is a widely used indicator that identifies the trend direction and determines support and resistance levels. It makes the trend clearer by filtering out the random price fluctuations.

Stochastic, created by George Lane while president of Investment Educators, are used to predict future price movements. They are based on the fact that as prices increase, closing prices tend to be closer to the upper end of the price range and in downtrends the closing price tends to be near the lower end of the range. To apply the theory, examine the most recent closing prices for the chosen time period, such as five days.

Rate of change measures the percentage change between the most recent price and the price of periods in the past. ROC is classed as a price momentum indicator or a velocity indicator because it measures the rate of change or the strength of momentum of change, scaling the difference in the trend.

Picking the right means of analysis can be a challenge. There is not one way, one analysis that always works best for all types of stocks, ETFs, or mutual funds. Recall, I have found that when investing in ETFs, relative strength momentum with or without standard deviation or alpha produce the best results. With stocks I usually find that relatives strength momentum or return, again with or without standard deviation, produce the best results. For mutual funds, I have found that alpha, alpha with standard deviation, or relative strength momentum gives the best profits.

The settings of these means of analysis, however, differ according to the type of ticker symbols in the group that is being analyzed. I have never found one particular setting that works for all the different types of groups I have analyzed. This makes back-testing imperative to find the best settings and the best means of analysis for any group of funds, ETFs, or stocks.

Personally, I have used alpha as my favorite means of analysis for many years. But recently I decided to test return to see which one would produce the best results. I ran tests from 1999 and from 2005 to the present. You might say I did a test drive to see if another model car would outperform the car I own.

Quite frankly I was amazed at the superb performance provided by return, especially when I incorporated a market exit signal into the analysis to pull me out of the markets when the S&P 500 was tanking. However, the alpha test drive still outperformed the return so I am sticking with my alpha method of relative strength analysis.

More About Winning with Technical Analysis

Using technical analysis is a surefire way to make the best choices and all you need is a software program that will do the job for you. Obviously you want a program that has a proven, reliable track record. Such technical analysis software will easily give you double digit gains and out-perform the S&P 500 or the Dow Jones.

In *Safe Profitable Investing with Relative Strength*, Michael J. Carr, a chartered market technician (CMT), thoroughly examined technical analysis by delving into the nitty-gritty. The first part of his book, which is admittedly a bit dry, explains and tests formulas based on different theories and concepts over different time frames. He also talks about investing in ETFs, mutual funds, and stocks so the book fits with whatever investment or diversification desires you may have.

One chart that Carr highly recommends is the *equity curve*. This is a moving average chart with both the fast and slow settings being identical. When the price line of the ticker symbol or the group being charted drops below the equity curve it is considered a signal to exit the strategy or the markets.

While Carr provides his readers with different formulas, he shows how investing based on relative strength will provide returns equal to your objectives. Using an alpha formula with a standard deviation component helps to reduce risk and provides an excellent means of analysis for a more conservative investment approach. Using just an alpha formula or relative strength momentum formula can be a more aggressive investment approach.

The key to technical analysis lies not in being a mathematician or even being an expert with Excel, but in finding user-friendly software that implements technical analysis; preferably software that doesn't require months to learn.

Keys to Safe Profitable Investing

There is software on the market that you can load onto your computer that will let you analyze stocks, ETFs, or mutual funds in a manner that matches both your tolerance for risk or potential losses and the amount of time you have for management. For example, by telling a software program like Dynamic Investor Pro that you prefer to hold your positions a minimum of 30 days you will limit your trading frequency dramatically compared to someone who says their preferred holding period is just five days.

With flexible investment software that you can tailor your strategies to fit your personality, your retirement goals and objectives so you can find safe investments. This will allow you to manage your retirement account and build your future security.

Again, it is equally important not to succumb to rumors, tips, or what someone *thinks* is going to happen or what may be a good buy. Sticking with good technical analysis, like one based on a type of relative strength, and following your strategies will lead to more success.

Using a software program that enables back testing I conducted a series of tests using a small group of ETFs. The group I used contained 12 sector ETFs and the S&P 500 (SPX) as the benchmark or comparison symbol.

I decided to keep my test somewhat simple although I could have added in more selling rules that could have made the results, the money earned, even better. I tested buy signals based on the alpha method of relative strength analysis, a ranking cutoff to maintain ownership in the best tickers, with the best purchase and trailing high stops the program recommended to provide the best results.

My key variable was how long I preferred to hold a position before selling. An important element regarding this factor is that it was a preference that could be over-ruled by the stops to prevent massive losses.

Comparisons were made between daily trading, weekly trading, monthly trading, and trading every few months as a preference. In all situations, even with wanting to trade just every few months there were times when the program had me trade more frequently in order to minimize losses.

The test period began with January 2005 and ended at the end of July 2011, a total of 79 months. I choose this time frame because the markets (as measured by the S&P 500), gyrated thru many ups and downs including the Great Recession in 2008 and its recovery.

The results were surprising.

	Portfolio Gain Possibilities	Trades	Trades/Month
Daily	118%–128%	228–595	2.88–7.53
Weekly	232%–243%	95–132	1.20–1.67
Monthly	224%–247%	53–94	0.67–1.19
Multiple Months	268%–301%	44–152	0.56–1.92

Take another look at these results. If you're concerned about your retirement account it's pretty obvious you don't have to be a daily trader. In fact being willing to review your portfolio on a weekly basis to catch sell signals may be the best approach and the most profitable. Even if you only want to adjust your portfolio occasionally as with the monthly or every few months trading concept it is still best to check things once a week to be sure you won't get burned by a market drop as happened to many retirement accounts during our recent Great Recession.

RELATIVE STRENGTH ANALYSIS

The basic concept of relative strength investing is not simply to buy an investment vehicle that is moving up in the markets but to buy one whose strength is greater than the others. A great way to use relative strength analysis is to combine it with momentum and selling rules so that you get the best of these worlds. By blending momentum with relative strength investing you will be more likely to buy the winners and also more likely to sell and preserve profits while minimizing losses.

Relative strength (RS) is a proven, successful way to analyze and select stocks, funds, or ETFs. Almost all investors base their decisions on some type of momentum, some indication that a ticker symbol is now or will soon be going up. The challenge here, even with a variety of charts, is to what degree the stock will rise.

RS analysis, of which alpha is one means of calculation, can be used to predict changes. Because the analysis, or predictions, are calculating the relative differences between the ETF or stock symbols in your group the potential for accuracy and stronger profits are greater. This compelling RS analysis focuses on ticker symbols that are strong and have the potential to not just remain strong but to continue rising; and when they falter, the analysis signals it's time to sell.

Benefits of Relative Strength Investing

The top benefits of using relative strength momentum investing are often overlooked in the desire to simply buy and make money.

- RS is one of the most proven methods of technical analysis for finding consistent winning investments.
- RS works for all types of investing.
- The formulas that provide the best results can be implemented even if you are not technically savvy or a math expert because they are part and parcel of readily available investment software.
- Analyzing investments with alpha or any of the other RS methods can be easily combined with other buy-sell rules in both personal investment software and investment advisor software.
- You can do easy technical analysis with or without standard deviation (SD). By adding SD to the analysis you can, in effect, automatically be more conservative. Actually, with or without SD you can optimize any RS calculation like alpha to meet your goals for conservative or moderate or even aggressive investing with the right investment software.

How Relative Strength Investing Wins in Turbulent Markets

Relative strength investing techniques can be profitable during all markets, especially when the markets are turbulent as in the past few years. The results you can expect when the markets are swinging depend upon how you approach RS and the particular formulas you select. In my experience and from extensive testing I have found that certain formulas generally provide the best results.

Best formulas for ETFs in order of performance are:

- relative strength momentum with standard deviation
- relative strength momentum
- alpha

Best formulas for stocks in order of performance are:

- relative strength momentum
- relative strength momentum with standard deviation
- return

Best formulas for mutual funds in order of performance are:

- alpha
- alpha with standard deviation
- relative strength momentum

The bottom line question is what kind of results you can expect. But safe investing with relative strength requires more than just the RS analysis. You might say RS alone is just one ingredient in the safe investing package. Without optimized buy-sell rules covering

117

specific trading factors of your group of potential investments you might as well just throw a dart at your list of stocks or funds.

In a nutshell, proper relative strength investing will return outstanding results, excellent growth, and profits for both retirement accounts and regular wealth building investment accounts. The caveat however, is that RS must be used as part of an overall package. While RS is the centerpiece, like a quarterback in a football game or a pitcher in baseball, the complete team is required to produce a winning investment strategy.

The complete package in any good investment software will also have ingredients such as stops, ranking, hold periods, time period of analysis, and a market exit signal.

Keys to Setting up Relative Strength Investing

Configuring a relative strength investment strategy to produce profitable investment results requires more than simply picking a method and plugging in typical, common settings. Results that produce safe investing with regular profits, regular gains, requires settings that meet the needs of the group and your objectives.

Type of relative strength. There are different types of relative strength analysis (RS) and these are often more suited to one type of investment or objective. For example, are your objectives aggressive or conservative or somewhere in-between; short-term or long-term; and are you investing from a group of stocks, ETFs, or mutual funds.

Aggressiveness. Generally speaking, an analysis based upon alpha is more aggressive than one based upon the normal relative strength momentum, return, or price oscillation. Yet, if you add standard deviation to alpha the result is a conservative to moderate analysis trading strategy. Aggressiveness, however, doesn't always produce the best results.

Objectives. If your objective is conservative or moderate growth with minimal risk to your money, then an investment strategy method of analysis that also uses standard deviation coupled with a market exit signal will give you adequate growth while protecting you when the market declines.

Testing and Settings

How you test or back-test your groups of ticker symbols and different types of analysis is critical.

If you are more aggressive and willing to trade frequently, almost daily versus weekly or occasionally then you will want to test with shorter time periods. Shorter time periods will give you signals for every twist and turn of the markets and your holdings but result in frequent trading that may or may not produce greater gains than more moderate trading based on weekly or monthly analysis.

Using your investment software and back-testing you can find strategies based upon gains coupled with losses that meet your goals. For example, an alpha 10 strategy—based on analysis of 10 trading days on a continual basis—will pick up every up and down movement as compared to an alpha 60 based on analysis of 60 trading days that which averages out the ups and down, resulting in less frequent trading.

A relative strength momentum analysis set with a fast 10 and slow 30 will act like the alpha 10 whereas settings of a fast 40 and slow 90 would be somewhat similar to the alpha 60. Note that results between alpha and RSM will be different because of how the different analysis themselves are computed.

Other factors in your strategy settings that also affect the results besides just the type of analysis include:

- desired frequency of analysis
- desired minimum hold periods indicating your preference for how long you want to keep a position as a minimum
- stops

The point is, just saying you are going to use relative strength investing is good, but only the beginning. Just as the same size shoe doesn't fit everyone, nor does the same shoe style work for everyone, there is not one-size fits all RS settings. Only after knowing what your objectives are and what type of investments you want to make, can you then test to find the settings that will work best for your group, your 401k, or any other group of funds, ETFs, or stocks.

CHAPTER 12: SELLING – YOU MUST SELL

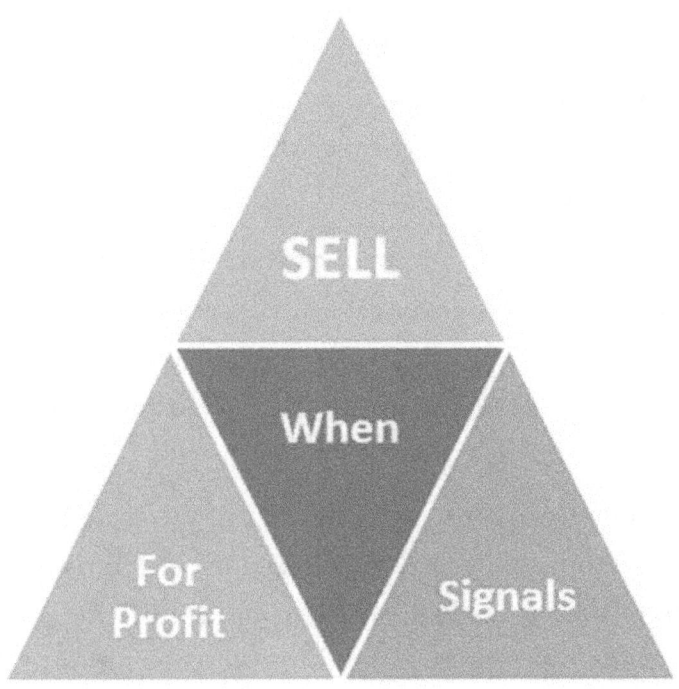

Profitable investing requires selling. A fund or ETF may be worth more on paper than it was when you bought it, but until you actually sell it, there is no real profit. But the key to your investment's profitability will depend on when you sell. Too often we let either emotions or our search for the best answer confuse us or lead us into a land of doubt, but there are a number of distinct scenarios that should trigger selling a stock or mutual fund.

Protecting Your Investments with Stops

One of the more common ways to determine when to sell is to implement stop orders, which is an order to buy or sell a security when its price surpasses a particular point to ensure a predetermined exit price, limiting the investor's loss or locking in their profit. You have a choice between using a set dollar figure or a sliding figure based on percentage. While the main reason many people use stops is to protect against losses, I like to think of stops as having three functions.

Stops lock in my profits so that when an ETF starts to drop from its high point I still make money. I'll get a sell signal or automatic trade based on the percentage drop from the greatest high the ETF reached since I purchased it.

Stops prevent me from losing too much money when I set a stop below my purchase price. I may want a 3 to 5 percent stop below what I paid for the stock so if it tumbles my risk is limited to just that amount.

Stops help control my trading frequency if I set them based on the type of group the position comes from and how often I prefer to trade. In other words a tight stop of just a few percentage points is going to result in more frequent trading while a higher number, say 7 to 9 percent will result in fewer trades and perhaps less volatility in my portfolio.

The other advantage of this process includes that you place stop orders on your investments based on your strategy rules. This helps you to lock in profits and minimize losses.

Influences

Stops have numerous influences besides just being a point at which you may sell a position. The personality of your strategy or group and the characteristics of the individual ticker symbol can impact what setting can or should be used. An ETF or ETF group strategy that bounces around a lot but within a tight range would lead you to frequent and possibly unnecessary trading if you had tight stops of 2, 3, or even 4 percent whereas stops of 6 percent to 9 percent will still allow you to lock in profits but avoid the frequent trades from erratic movements within an upward climb.

If however, you want to trade frequently, minimize risk, and make money on small profits then tight stops make absolute sense.

There is a pitfall to using automatic stops that kick in with your broker. There is no guarantee your position will actually sell at your stop price because if the markets are extremely volatile or there is a shortage of buyers you could find yourself selling for a substantially lower amount then your stop setting. This is why some investors simply have their investment program give them sell signals which can be based partially on stops so they can pick the time to sell.

In any event, to totally ignore stops would be dangerous because you are putting your investments at total risk without any warning device to help you preserve your original money or your profits.

There are two types of stops. A purchase stop means when the price of your symbol drops a certain amount from what you paid for it, you sell.

A trailing stop is set at a certain percentage or a certain dollar amount below the market price. This type of stop is a way to automatically protect yourself from an investment's downside while locking in the upside.

For example, suppose you buy Company XYZ for $10 and decide that you don't want to lose more than 5 percent on your investment but want to be able to take advantage of any price increases. You also don't want to have to constantly monitor your trades to lock in gains so you set a trailing stop on XYZ that orders you to sell if the price dips more than 5 percent below the market price.

The benefits of the trailing stop are two-fold. First, if the stock moves against you, the trailing stop will trigger when XYZ hits $9.50, protecting you from a great loss. But if the stock goes up to $20, the trigger price for the trailing stop comes up with it, meaning the trailing stop will now only trigger a sale if the stock drops below $19. This helps you lock in most of the gains from the stock's rally. You could also decide you don't want to lose more than $2 on your $10 investment. If the stock goes up to $20, the trailing stop would follow the price and only trigger if the stock falls to $18.

A trailing stop can be good for investors who may not have enough discipline to lock-in gains or cut losses. It removes some of the emotion from the trading process and offers some automatic capital protection.

But there are some drawbacks to consider. If you have invested in a somewhat volatile stock and have a relatively low trailing stop percentage or amount, the stop level could be triggered fairly often. Also, frequent trading can have tax implications as well as have fees and commissions eating into your profits.

Most investment authors generally recommend setting stops based on percent, with typical recommendations around 7–8 percent. Some investment software programs allow you to perform back-testing that can then tell you what stop settings to use to achieve the best results based on the group of funds, stocks, or ETFs you may be using for your group.

Every stock or fund goes down at some point so by setting stops you protect your retirement account from dramatic losses and ensure you will make a profit when a position starts to go down. Without stops you can suffer dramatic losses, as many did during the Great Recession of 2008. Following principles of safe investing using stops and making new decisions at a regular time will not only protect your money but keep you on a safe investment course of strong profitability.

Selling Doesn't Always Require a New Buy

Selling a stock or mutual fund does not mean you always have to buy a new one immediately. Part of the key to using stops is to not panic or wonder what to do when your positions sell when your stops kick in. The best course is to make your next decisions in the same time frame and the same way as you normally do. In other words, if you look at your portfolio weekly, then even if your stops caused a position to sell on Tuesday, wait until your normal review time on Saturday to decide whether or not to buy a new fund or to just let your money sit in cash for a while.

If you examine your portfolio or retirement account every day and a position sells out mid-day, the principle is the same as if it were a weekly strategy. Wait until your normal time to update your strategy and then make a decision on what, if anything, to purchase.

By waiting until your normal time you will achieve three results:

- less stress
- your buy decision will be based on your normal process
- you will better know if it is even time to buy or take a break from investing

By following your normal process of evaluating buy/sell recommendations from your investment software you can avoid:

- making a buy decision based on yesterdays or last weekend's information
- being sure your software doesn't give a market exit signal
- rushing a decision

Also, by waiting until your normal time to evaluate your investments you will not suddenly, or worse, repeatedly find yourself exceeding the amount of time you want to spend managing your retirement or wealth accounts. In this way you won't get discouraged and decide you don't have the time to handle your future and give up the potential to grow your portfolio.

Specific Percentage Drop

A number of authors suggest setting a trailing stop at 7 percent or 8 percent so if your stock goes up and then starts down you automatically sell it if it drops this specific percent from its highest value. This sounds simple and precise. But what about those days that occur every so often during the year when the entire market cascades down for one or even three days only to bounce back up?

If your philosophy is to sell based solely on specific percentage drop, then you really need to bite the bullet and sell. If the market does rebound, or even before it starts climbing back up, you should buy what is on your watch list of stocks or funds that you are interested in but can't buy because your money was already fully invested.

Chart Signals

You can get good signals from charts if you understand how to read them. Some charts give pretty straight forward buy/sell signals while others can show a ticker in between a buy and sell point leading to either the buy or sell indication.

But the most challenging aspect of using charts revolves around two factors.

Which charts to use. Some chart program offer more than one hundred varieties. If you look at more than two or three charts you can end up spending hours or even all day studying them only to discover that some say *buy,* some say *hold,* and some may say *sell*—all for the same stock on the same day. My answer to this dilemma is to pick and concentrate on just two or three charts and don't look at others because you then set yourself up for confusion, which leads to doubt, not taking action, and invariably leads to losing money.

What settings to use. Most chart programs come with default settings, which might be based on some long-ago investor's philosophy that is usually based on his risk level and how long he generally wants to hold a position. Your settings should be based on *your* level of risk and how often *you* prefer to trade so the signals help you achieve your goals. This may involve asking questions, but that is a good thing because then your chart settings will fit you.

Investment Program Signal

Most investor software programs give precise buy/sell signals and some allow you to set the parameters for buying and selling. This makes it easy if you stick with the program and the signals. The challenge comes when we want to see if we'd get better results if we changed the parameters.

The key to using an investment program is to follow or develop trading strategies that can be back-tested and then stick with them. Looking at alternatives within the program negates the strategy, your back-testing, and the optimized strategy. Unless your program offers a verification method to confirm the recommendations, just looking around for another recommendation invalidates your entire process and puts you back into the realm of emotional decision making.

Ultimately the best answer for when to sell or hold an ETF or mutual fund is to follow a specific sell/hold method that you accept and stick with at all times.

Keys to Selling and Maximizing Profits

Knowing when and why to sell can be hard, particularly if you become emotionally attached to your holdings. But if you follow set selling rules you will maximize your profits and minimize any investment losses.

The key to unemotional selling is to have rules or parameters that when met require you to sell your investment. Such rules include, but are not limited to:

- Decline. The stock goes down a certain percent or a certain dollar amount.

- Drop in rank. The ETF is part of a group and after owning it a while it is no longer ranked at the top by your means of analysis and is now below a certain level.

- Chart signal. The signal based on your chart of choice is to sell.

- General exit signal. A chart or calculation that analyzes the strength of the markets and this benchmark gives an exit the market signal.

- Rebalance. Automatically sell at certain times of the year or after a certain number of months so you then buy the current best performers.

With strong sell rules you will lock in profits and minimize losses.

Market Exit Signal Choices

A declining market is the greatest challenge and test for all investors and there are certain actions you can take when the market heads downward.

Cashing out requires reading the signals that have a tendency to predict the best time to exit the markets. One of the strongest exit signals is the equity curve of the S&P 500 with a setting of 100 days. Other cash out signals could be when the equity curve of a group trading strategy gives the signal or when both the moving average and the full stochastic chart are all in sell mode. Another technical analysis signal would be if the ticker symbols of the group are all ranked below the benchmark or S&P.

Investing for the long-term means you are willing to ride out a market drop because of the overall future strength of your holdings. The market in decline can be a good time to buy such positions whether they are individual stocks, ETFs, or mutual funds. Besides future growth capability, these holdings will produce dividend income that can be automatically reinvested so your portfolio continues to grow and is ready to surge when the markets again go up.

Short-term signals can be generated using technical analysis. This may mean switching to a different set of strategies for your investment groups. Analyzing relative strength with an alpha period of 10 continual trading days or even 30 will be more responsive to market changes than if you are analyzing based on trading periods of 60 or 90 continual trading days.

Also, if your group contains one to four Treasury ETFs or similar bond funds, and your analysis indicates these are the best choice, you have received a signal to move out of the markets and have the option of going to cash or actually purchasing the Treasury, ETF, or bond funds.

The most difficult aspect is to actually follow through to exit the market when these signals are given. Human nature is generally optimistic so we don't want to sell. Don't be ruled by emotion; sell and lock in your profits when the sell exit signals are generated.

When and Why to Rebalance Your Investment Portfolio

The concept of rebalance means to sell your stocks, mutual funds, or ETFs and buy new positions as if you were starting all over in the stock market. In relation to safe investing, rebalancing means that you are going to sell all or most of your positions at a specific point in time and pick new investments that offer less risk than your present holdings.

When to rebalance your portfolio depends on your investment philosophy. Some investment advisors advocate quarterly rebalancing while others suggest it is only necessary once a year. An investment program may offer you the opportunity to set up automatic rebalancing at pre-determined times like monthly, quarterly, semi-annually, or yearly.

The advantages of rebalancing include:

- Poor performing positions are eliminated.

- Positions with greater potential, either for minimal risk or greater profit are purchased.

- You can balance out the value of your positions equally so your diversification level remains constant and equal.

There are also potential disadvantages, such as:

- You could sell a highly profitable position that is still growing.

- Your trading expense may grow needlessly.

- Automatic rebalancing at specific times may turn out to be the wrong time to sell.

It's not a bad idea to take a look at your portfolio, strategies, and positions annually or perhaps even every six months to see how your chosen strategies are doing compared to your watch strategies. In other words perhaps your rebalance should be to switch strategies and positions.

CHAPTER 13: TIMING SIGNALS

Timing signals are a way for investors to trade the stock market when conditions are the most favorable. Most markets create trading trends or patterns. Timing signals allow investors and traders to be in the market in up trends, and out of the market as it weakens and starts to trend down. Following simple market timing signals can dramatically improve your trading success.

Popular Signals – Let's Review Once More

The essence with everything concerning investing, especially safe investing for your retirement, revolves around timing—when should you sell, when should you buy. There are many types of timing signals.

Technical strategies. One of the most popular market timing signals, technical analysis studies the movement and change in a stock price and its volume...

Fundamental analysis deals with researching the financial health of a company in relation to its stock price. One of the most popular fundamental signal tools is the P/E ratio, which is a stock's price divided by its earnings per share.

Economic reports are used by some traders who look at federal and private reports on employment, home sales, inflation index, consumer sentiment, and actions by the Federal Reserve.

Software. Many investment programs offer analysis of popular market timing tools and indicators as well as custom programming options so that you can create your own custom timing indicators, and have the ability to back-test trading results.

A word of caution: just because a stock is moving up doesn't mean it is the best stock to own from your group of stocks. There may be another stock that is moving up faster. Along that line, a mutual fund you are holding may be moving up very slowly and may not trigger any sell rules because its slow growth may still equal safe growth and the other funds in your group may be going down or showing erratic up/down moves. Back-testing and customizing of your buy/sell rules will help you develop the best strategy for each of your investment groups.

The advantage of using a variety of buy/sell rules is simple: instead of relying upon just one signal for when to buy or sell you can have a number of rules that can be back-tested to give the best results based upon the exact group of symbols you are working with, maximizing your returns while maintaining a safe investing procedure.

Equity curve. As discussed by Michael Carr in *Safe Profitable Investing with Relative Strength,* an equity curve can provide a buy/sell signal for individual symbols and strategies. As I have said, this curve is similar to a moving average chart but focusing on the trends of a symbol can tell you if it is a good buy, better to hold, or if it is time to sell. The same goes for a strategy based upon a universe of symbols.

In addition there is the equity curve of an index like the S&P 500. I actually look at both the equity curves for each of my individual strategies and an equity curve for the market as a whole based on the S&P 500 index. When the markets are in a general upward movement setting the moving average parameters at 250 trading days for each works well. But when the markets are crazy turbulent I set the parameters at 100 each.

With an equity curve in place an exit signal is easy to see. Quite simply, with this technique, when the price line of the strategy or the index cuts down through the smooth equity curve line it is time to either stop using that strategy or completely get out of the markets.

The critical aspect, as any investor knows, is buying and selling at the right time defines whether or not you are going to make money or lose money. By employing timing signals instead of feelings or tips you are more likely to reach or surpass your goals and make more money.

Market Timing vs. Buy and Hold

Some experts consider market timing to be little more than a guessing game and advocate simply buying and holding good stocks. The problem with anti-market timing arguments is that they always focus on tracking particular ticker symbols and question the ability to buy or sell that one symbol at the right time. The advantage with some software is that they can tell you when a ticker is going down and when another ticker is outperforming your current holding, even if your current holding is still going up. This ability, this power means that losses are limited by your sell rules and gains become cumulative so as to far surpass results from simply holding an individual ticker.

The folly with taking a buy/hold approach has been fully illustrated with the 2008 Great Recession when retirees following the buy/hold philosophy lost 40-60 percent of the value of their portfolios. While many portfolios recouped a lot of their value when the markets swung up from the recession lows, imagine where they would be today if they had sold at the beginning of the recession to minimize their losses and then saw their retirement portfolio grow when the markets surged after the recession.

I know the recession hit my portfolio but not nearly as badly as most others because the software I was using told me to sell and move to cash. The same software then told me to buy just as the markets were swinging up so my gains were based on about the same value as before the crash.

In other words, buy and hold means your stocks and your portfolio are going to move like a rollercoaster ride. While I like riding the Space Mountain roller coaster at Disney World, I would rather my portfolio traced a route more like going on a scenic drive along a valley floor that has a few ups and downs but is basically moving on a constant upward path toward a high mountain ridge.

The key for your retirement account is not simply market timing, but rather to picking positions that are moving ahead better than others, even better than what your current holding is doing. This is accomplished by:

- relative strength analysis using alpha or relative strength momentum

- sell signals based on stops, ranking level, and market movement

- selling to strength, limiting losses, and exiting the market when risk becomes too great

With flexible investment software you can tailor your strategies to fit your personality, your goals, and objectives so you can find safe investments. This will allow you to manage your retirement account and build your future security.

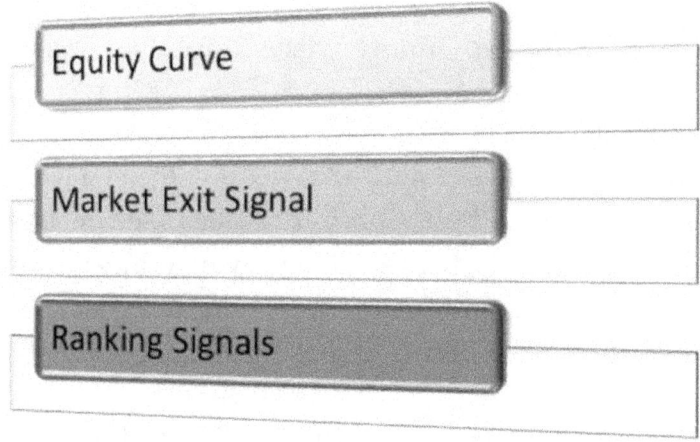

Eliminating risk; that's a key to safe investing. In fact if it weren't for "risk" more people, perhaps you, would be active stock market investors.

But "risk" needs to be kept in perspective.

Remember what President Franklin D. Roosevelt said, "the only thing we have to fear is fear itself."

If you are scared of risk perhaps you should ask yourself a few questions:

- Do you drive a car? Do you ride in a car? There is risk in car driving or even riding, that's why there are insurance companies and auto body repair businesses – because there is risk.

- What about deer? Deer are cute and loveable but I wrecked one car when a deer jumped out in front of me. When I spoke with my insurance company, the lady, who lives in Texas, remarked how often she is scared to drive her few miles to work because there are so many deer and so many deer-caused accidents. Risk.

- Here in Montana people hike with bear spray on their belt. Why? Because of bears, especially grizzly bears. They even make a short hike risky; but the trails in Glacier National Park are jam packed with hikers (and sometimes bears). Risk.

- Heck, some of the most common accidents happen at home: slipping in the bath tub, falling down stairs, burning a finger on a hot pan. Risk.

I doubt you can even avoid risk by living in a bubble.

The important fact to keep in mind is simply that risk always exists in everything, everywhere, always. But risk does not equal fear. With the best investment tools risk can be reduced to almost nothing and fear eliminated so that anyone can enjoy safe profitable investing. This means you, anyone, can grow your income, build a retirement account safely and profitably without worrying about losing your hard earned money.

Taking action before your investments are at risk is the key to not just a conservative investment strategy but to any investing. Unless you are a day trader, your investments are at risk to a variety of calamities including war, terrorism, natural disasters, changing regulatory policies, and even bad news about companies you have invested with, such as when *Consumer Reports* gave Tesla a D rating, resulting in an immediate 10 percent drop in the auto maker's stock prices.

One method to protect your investments and your complete retirement portfolio is to always play it safe and confine yourself to conservative investments. But following that investment philosophy will limit your ability to grow your money. A moderate investment strategy will usually provide both safety and strong gains. You may miss out on some of the rapidly rising stars but you are also less likely to experience major losses.

A principle of investing is to minimize drawdown, the percentage your portfolio drops at any one time or between the market highs and the lows. If you invest with the buy and hold philosophy you will most likely experience dramatic drawdowns over the course of time, and while your portfolio may recover from these losses, if you need to cash out part or all of your money in the midst of these drops, you will suffer big money losses. This is especially important with a traditional IRA when you have to withdraw a minimum amount every year after you reach 70 years old; especially if you are depending upon your retirement account for monthly income. Thus the underlying fault of the buy and hold concept.

The alternative is a willingness to trade and take profits, cut losses to a minimum, and buy at the best opportunity. With a good investment software program you should be able to set buy/sell rules to help you reduce risk. Some of these rules may give you signals for when to simply get out of the markets, while others will help you avoid massive or even medium size losses.

Protecting Your Automated Investment Strategy

Investment strategies can give you buy/sell signals based on your method of analysis and chosen buy-sell rules. But one common question is whether or not having a money market fund in the group would protect you when the market declines.

The investment program I use does not include money market funds in the database because money market funds don't really trade. Their price stays at $1 all the time so if they ever jump in rank to the top of a strategy they would stay there forever. One alternative is to use an ETF that mimics a money market or an ETF for a stable bond group.

So how do you protect your investments, your investment strategies?

The market exit signal (ME) in some investment programs is specifically designed to tell you when to exit the markets. I use it in almost all of my strategies. My back-testing indicates that if someone used an ME investing tool with the benchmark option they would have experienced minimal losses during the 2008 Great Recession and moved back into the markets almost immediately when the markets began their climb back up.

In essence the best way to protect your automated investment analysis buy/sell recommendations is to:

· choose a market exit signal

- check the equity curve of your positions
- check the equity curve of the market (S&P 500)

The use of one of these signals or even all three should help you reduce losses to the bare bone minimums.

ReCap – Three Ways to Avoid Market Crashes

How many times have you seen the markets crash and watched portfolios shrink? Before the market dives there are three methods that can help you preserve your cash:

Equity curve is not about making money. It indicates it is either time to switch strategies, switch to a different group of ticker symbols, or move to cash or bonds to safeguard your retirement money.

Benchmark exit signal is similar to an equity curve or moving average but is based strictly on the performance of a major index such as the S&P 500, Dow Jones, or NASDAQ. The signal is based on equity curve. Again, a setting of 100 trading days has consistently moved me out of the markets prior to major crashes.

Ticker rank plus combo charts. The first element of this method is to see where the ticker symbol of your holdings or potential buys stands in comparison to the performance of the benchmark in your group of tickers. The next step is to examine two key charts: moving average and full stochastic. Both of these charts should be giving out buy signals if you are going to buy the particular position. If the ticker ranks below the S&P 500 and both charts are giving sell signals then the best

143

course is to protect yourself by either moving to cash or bonds.

These three methods will enable you to avoid losing large chunks of your portfolio. You can either employ all three or just one or two to protect yourself.

Getting Back In

Getting back into the market after you have moved all or most of your portfolio to cash requires both a plan and patience. Being impatient can put your portfolio at risk.

The two most common worries are whether you are getting back in too early or too late and whether you should invest immediately or space it out. The answer is to trust the method of investing you have been using. If you are using an investment software program to analyze and provide buy/sell signals and it has been successful for you in the past, then wait for new buy signals.

How much to invest should also be based on buy signals. If you sold six positions, you will most likely buy back in with six new symbols. But unless your methodology gives you six unique buy signals on the same day you will most likely just buy as the signals come, and this could take weeks or even months before you are fully invested again. You might miss opportunities by waiting for your signals but sticking with your methods will also reduce risk and be more likely to garner future gains. Because different groups of ticker symbols react different to market forces it is most likely that new buy signals will be spread out over time; but this is a good things as it helps keep you diversified and reduces risk.

In other words, if your investment methods have been building your retirement account, then the safest course is to continue your analysis at the same frequency and move back in as your methodology suggests. Changing methods of analysis at this point can put you in the position of using unproven methods to make your investment decisions.

I find that it takes me a few months to get back to being fully invested. Yes, it is frustrating at times, but I just keep reminding myself it is safer to jump in with a positive signal rather than to just jump in not knowing what the outcome will be. And I want my retirement account to grow. I am sure you do to.

Rise Above the Crowd

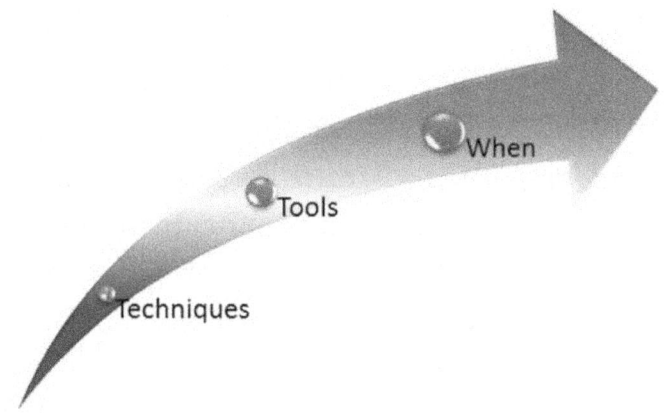

Don't be swayed, stick with your plan. Once you have a solid, proven winner for your retirement investment plan it is important, if not critical that you stick with it.

A good plan is just like preparing dinner:

- Figure out what you want...stocks, ETFs, or funds
- Check the ingredients...Which group of stocks or funds or ETFs
- Do some research for the best recipe...Method of analysis, back-test to find the best strategies
- Prep time...how much time do you have to develop your strategies
- Cooking time...How much time and how often to manage your investments

Consistency with a retirement investment plan doesn't mean buy something until you or the stock dies. Consistency in an investment plan means developing a plan based on a recognized means of analysis like relative strength momentum or alpha with a variety of tested sell signals and perhaps even a signal for when it is time to take a pause and exit the markets entirely.

If you create a plan with half a dozen different groups in your retirement portfolio and for each group you have two or three strategies you will achieve both diversification and a strong degree of safety. By the way, if you are working with a 401k you can sub-divide your investment choices into groups for better and easier management and greater profit.

Now you have a retirement focused investment plan you can stick with because:

- It is based on your personality.
- It is formed with your time constraints in mind.
- It is aimed directly at your own objectives.
- It consists of stocks or ETFs or funds that you are willing to consider.
- It has strategies back-tested for both buying and selling.

It is important in creating your groups to settle on not just one strategy but to have two or three trading strategies for each group. Experience says that switching from one strategy to another can be advisable because frequently one will perform better than the other depending upon the economic climate.

One strategy may be better in volatile markets while another may excel in stable markets. Thus by having a few strategies for each group you don't have to self-guess what is best in today's market; your strategies will tell you, plain and simple. And when they tell you what to do, it is a lot easier to stick with your plan and not be swayed by your emotions, the news, or your neighbor.

With this retirement plan you won't have to worry about your financial future. You will have covered your own back.

CREDITS, REFERENCES, REFERRALS

Dynamic Investor Pro investment software was used with permission for back-testing and analysis for various results mentioned throughout this book.

A few popular brokerages with excellent on-line websites:

Fidelity	http://personal.fidelity.com
eTrade	https://us.etrade.com
TD Ameritrade	www.tdameritrade.com
CharlesSchwab,	www.schwab.com
Scottrade,	www.scottrade.com

Other books worth reading:

"Safe Profitable Investing with Relative Strength", by Michael Carr and Raymond Dominick.

Available on Amazon in both print and as an eBook

Investment Software:

Dynamic Investor Pro
http://www.dynamicinvestorpro.com/

Special Offer for all investors
http://www.dynamicinvestorpro.com/standard-special

Special Offer for Professional Advisors
http://www.dynamicinvestorpro.com/advisor-special

About the Author

Raymond M.F. Dominick has been investing in the markets since he was a teenager. He began by using his mother's account while attending Taft High School in Chicago. A graduate of the University of Montana, School of Journalism; he was awarded a three-year Kellogg Fellowship to study leadership and community development in the United States and the People's Republic of (mainland) China. His career has taken him from Chicago to all parts of the globe. In his later years, he became a registered Investment Advisor Representative (IAR), a career he enjoyed for many years.

In between his first stock investments and prior to his IAR, Raymond was a business writer for national magazines and general manager for a variety of businesses in a career that spanned more than 30 years.

In 2008 Raymond designed the software program Dynamic Investor Pro for both novice and professional investors alike. He currently serves as CEO of Dynamic Investing, LLC—the publisher of the software program. Dynamic Investing, LLC is headquartered just a short commute from Glacier National Park— Raymond's resource for stress release and inspiration.

Other Books include:
  Invest Safely and Profitably, 2014

www.ingramcontent.com/pod-product-compliance
Lightning Source LLC
Chambersburg PA
CBHW051510170526
45166CB00001B/471